A
CARDIFF
Anthology

A
CARDIFF
Anthology

Selected by Meic Stephens

SEREN BOOKS
1987

Seren Books is an imprint of Poetry Wales Press
56 Parcau Avenue, Bridgend, Mid Glamorgan

British Library Cataloguing in Publication Data

A Cardiff anthology,
   1. Welsh literature—Translations into
   English 2. English Literature—
   Translations from Welsh
   I. Stephens, Meic
   891.6′608   PB2361

ISBN 0-907476-84-8

Published with the support of HTV Wales

Cover Design: Jeane Rees
Cover Illustration: 'Royal Arcade' by Falcon D. Hildred
(Private Collection)
Photography: Andrew Knight Gallery

Printed in 10pt Baskerville by
by J.W. Arrowsmith Ltd., Bristol

CONTENTS

Preface

This book is an anthology of writing about Cardiff, the capital of Wales. As cities go, Cardiff is not very old. Towards the end of the eighteenth century it was only a small market-town, with about two thousand inhabitants. Its development over the next fifty years was largely due to the Bute family, who built a canal, docks and a railway for the transport of coal and iron from the valleys of Glamorgan, and thereafter its growth was rapid. By 1901, with a population of some 164,000, Cardiff had become the largest town in Wales and the greatest coal port in the world. Granted the status of a city in 1905 — its splendid civic centre dates from about the same year — it was officially declared the capital of Wales in 1955. Since then its population has continued to grow, to nearly 280,000 by today, while its role in the commercial, cultural and political life of Wales is now well established.

In view of Cardiff's brief history as a place of any size or consequence, it was to be expected that most of the verse and prose to be published in *A Cardiff Anthology* would be by writers born during the present century. Only one author, namely Jack Jones, has written extensively about Cardiff prior to 1900, and his novel *River out of Eden* (1951) remains the best fictional account of its first hundred years as a metropolis. The rest deal mainly with life in Cardiff from its Edwardian heyday through the recession of the inter-war years to the city's return to prosperity in our own time. The book's contents are arranged in roughly chronological order, according to the period in which they are set.

Almost all districts are featured, from notorious Tiger Bay to the academe of Rhiwbina, and some vivid glimpses are provided into both the low life and the high, the intimate and the public, the light-hearted and the serious. It may be that no such thing as a distinctive 'Cardiff voice' is to be heard in these pages (the famous accent is another matter), yet it might be said that, disparate though our writers are, the peculiarly bitter-sweet experience of living in the city has left an indelible mark on most of them. It is, of course, up to the reader to detect in what ways that might be true, but I venture to suggest that, on the whole, they take an affectionate, if sometimes sardonic, view of place and people, and that it is usually those not 'Cardiff born and Cardiff bred' who chide the city for not being what they would have it be. Even so, the animus often has a wit and sympathy which raise the writing above mere invective.

Only about a third of the authors represented are natives of Cardiff, but they include such distinguished figures as Howard Spring, Alun Llywelyn-Williams, Dannie Abse, Bernice Rubens and Bobi Jones, together with a number of younger writers like Gillian Clarke, Gilbert Ruddock, Duncan Bush, Peter Finch and Oliver Reynolds. As many again were either brought up in the city or have lived here so long that their eligibility for inclusion in *A Cardiff Anthology* seems to be beyond question. A glance at the contents list, and at the biographical notes at the rear of the book, will reveal who these writers are. It may surprise some readers to learn that Eric Linklater and Roald Dahl, both of whom enjoy reputations made elsewhere, were in fact born in the city's suburbs and spent their early years there. On the other hand, the absence of Maurice Edelman and Brian Morris, to name but two writers who seem not to have written much about their native city, is a matter for regret; the same is unfortunately true of John Ormond, for long a citizen of Cardiff, and some others. A rather more conspicuous gap may be attributed to my failure to find verse or prose by people from Cardiff's Asian and Afro-Caribbean communities. I looked hard, but discovered little and none that satisfied my principal criterion of literary merit.

For a similar reason I set aside the genre of personal reminiscence, as written by several Cardiffians in recent years: however authentic they may be (and some are of considerable interest), their charm seems to me essentially artless; and in any case, they are easily found elsewhere, most notably in the valuable series of *Cardiff Books* published by Mr Stewart Williams. Nor was there space for excerpts from the scholarly accounts of Cardiff's history written by such specialists as William Rees, John B. Hilling and John Davies. Nevertheless, I am confident that the net has been as widely cast as to ensure weight, flavour and variety enough to please most readers.

It remains for me to thank all the authors and their publishers for permission to reprint copyright material in this anthology, but especially those who kindly gave me advice in the selection and translation of their work. I am also grateful to Mr Mick Felton and Miss Angela Howells for their assistance in the task of compilation, to my wife Ruth for helping me with the proofs, and to HTV for contributing towards the cost of publication.

From the outset I have been aware that this book would be published, as it is now, exactly one hundred and fifty years after work began on the building of the first Bute Dock in 1837. It is my hope that such a happy coincidence will serve to remind the people of Cardiff, and of Wales, not only of the city's historical past but also of the vital part played by writers in the capital's cultural life today.

Meic Stephens
Whitchurch, Cardiff
September 1987

JACK JONES

A Dock in the Making

John Crichton Stuart, Second Marquess of Bute, descended from King Robert the Second of Scotland, was not finding much comfort in the sermon being delivered by the Vicar of St. John's Church, Cardiff. He sat in his pew feeling rather depressed and weighed down by his many titles, duties and responsibilities. Outside the Church his carriage and four, with coachman and footman, waited.

His lordship's chief worry this Sunday evening in the late summer of 1838 was a dock in the making, a dock which — so he and his agents had more than once stated — he was "making for Cardiff". Up to now the job had cost him about £200,000 sterling, and the materials supplied from his own estate: stone, timber, lime, etc., would have cost him at least another £200,000 had he had to go elsewhere to purchase them. It was a huge and costly undertaking, probably the greatest and most costly that any one man in Britain, noble or otherwise, had up to this time entered upon.

So when Daniel Storm, the contractor who had taken the job on from where Messrs. Dawson and Dalton had left off, appeared before his lordship about a fortnight previous, to inform him that the English navvies, most of whom were Yorkshiremen, had struck work to enforce their demand for higher wages, his lordship was at a loss for words.

"We're already paying them more by a ha'penny an hour than the contractors making that railway up into the hills are paying their navvies," said Daniel Storm. "Yet these men of ours are demanding another extra penny an hour."

"Outrageous!" exclaimed the Marquess. "Still, the contract is yours and so is this problem."

"Granted, my lord. Yet I can't afford any more than I'm now paying them. As it is I'm afraid I shall lose money on the job."

"I stand to lose hundreds of thousands and you come here to —". The Marquess checked himself. "But we mustn't lose our tempers. This is serious and may prove disastrous. If the job's left to stand for more than a week or so the damage and additional expense will be enormous. I simply couldn't stand it."

"Neither could I, my lord, it would ruin me."

"And almost ruin me — but haven't you anything to suggest?"

11

"Yes, my lord. Find me shipping and I'll find plenty of labour to be on the job in less than a fortnight from now. The sub-contractors and foremen between them will manage to keep the job in shape until then. Provide me with the ships and I'll bring a couple of hundred labourers over from Ireland."

"Ireland!" cried the Marquess.

"Yes, my lord. The rate we've been paying the men now on strike will attract all the labour we want from Ireland."

The great Protestant nobleman shuddered at the thought of two hundred Irish Catholics being imported, with his consent, to work on the dock on which he had already staked nearly the whole of his fortune. He shook his head and firmly said, "Never."

The contractor shrugged his shoulders and sighed. "Then what can we do, my lord?"

"Anything but what you suggest, Mr Storm. If, with my consent, you were to land two hundred Papists, I should be guilty of establishing Popery here at Cardiff. And once they got a footing here and by some means or other erected a Catholic church they and their priests would never rest until they dominated the spiritual life of the town. However, William Cubitt is coming to dinner this evening, when I'll have a word with him and my agent. My agent may be able to arrange for a supply of labour from the hills."

"I'm afraid not, my lord. The ironworks and collieries up in the hills need all the labour they've got and as much more as they can get. Besides, whatever labour we've got from that part wouldn't be easy to handle. I don't think that you need fear that Popery will rear its head here in Cardiff if we fetch enough Irish to break this strike. Another year's work and the dock will be finished, then we can scatter the Irish — drive them up into the hills. Forty years ago the Irish who worked on the making of the canal from here to Merthyr left no mark on the life of Cardiff. That was before your time, my lord, but I was here sub-contracting on that job. Anyway I don't need to remind you how urgent the matter is. After you've talked it over with William Cubitt and your estate agent this evening I'd be obliged if you'd let me know what I'm to do. If we're to prevent the job from being ruined then we must get at least a couple of hundred men from somewhere within a fortnight. Either that or we concede the demands the chaps on strike have made on us. As for myself, my lord, I can't meet that demand —".

"So you've already told me," said the Marquess irritably. "However,

I'll let you have my mind in the morning."

"Thanks, my lord. You may think differently after you've slept on it."

"It's more likely that I shall not. Good-day."

The contractor took his leave and the Marquess went to take tea with the Marchioness to whom he explained the situation. She was even more horrified than he was at the prospect of two hundred Irish Catholics being shipped to Cardiff to work on the dock which was by now generally known as the 'Bute Dock'.

"If it is imperative that labourers be brought here from Ireland couldn't they be got from the Protestant part of that country?" she asked.

"Possibly, my dear, I didn't think of that when the contractor was here; but from what I've gathered, the huge reservoir of labour is in the Catholic south of Ireland. When I think of all the difficulties we've already had to overcome — and this trouble again, I almost regret having embarked on the venture. But it was so necessary, both to the development of this town and the industries situated on my land up in the hills. The canal has for years past been too congested with traffic to allow for any further industrial development, and the canal lock here at Cardiff is altogether inadequate." He smiled and patted her hand. "Forgive me, my dear, for although it's a great comfort to be able to relieve my mind I shouldn't do it at the expense of your peace of mind."

"I wish I could help."

"You do, my dear, you do. A talk after dinner with William Cubitt and my agent may result in a solution. Cubitt's been a tower of strength. Now, if you'll excuse me, I'll go and see what my secretary has for me to sign before dinner."

from *River out of Eden* (1951)

13

HERBERT WILLIAMS

The Friend of Freedom

A statue set
within a shopping street,
a rather quaint inscription at his feet.

"John Batchelor, the friend
of freedom." Well,
he may have been some use, but what the hell?

And so we hurry past
this man of stone,
not caring what the fellow might have done,

ignoring all
the things he did when he
was blood and bone, not city deity.

John Batchelor, you knew
the ways of men,
and wouldn't be surprised that once again

the world has shown
it soon forgets the dead.
The friend of freedom. Pigeons on his head.

JACK JONES

A Daily Newspaper

What has he done? He has launched a daily newspaper, the first daily paper to be published for Wales and the West of England at Cardiff, and this venture alone may cost him a hundred thousand pounds and the friendship of many. For the *Western Mail* has come out in its true colours as a Conservative organ opposed to Mr Gladstone and his Ministry and Liberalism. This, in Cardiff, a town as overwhelmingly Liberal as the rest of Wales, was taken as an insult and the weekly *Cardiff Times*, the voice of Liberalism, on behalf of Liberalism angrily denounced this 'move' of the Castle into politics. "Disgraceful!" cried many a Cardiff Liberal, Mostyn Lewis leading the cry down at the docks. "With his uncle our Liberal member all these years Bute has the cheek to do this!"

"Colonel Stuart is not his uncle, is he?" said John Morgan, the ships' chandler.

"Whether or no, he's related to him," said Mostyn.

This relationship was not referred to in the after-dinner conversation at the Castle, a conversation of which the essence must be repeated after the barest mention of two other things which must be placed to Bute's credit or discredit, according to the way you look at it.

At a cost of ten thousand pounds he built a splendid Drill Hall for the Volunteers and closely associated himself with the new Volunteer movement. He also built a Convent near Cardiff Castle for the nuns which many spoke of as Sisters of Mercy.

Bute had in a Mr Burgess, a resident architect, whom he kept busy all the time. The architect lived in the Castle which he was all the time restoring and altering and renovating. With scores of skilled workmen at his command the work continued irrespective of its cost. Cardiff Castle and the Red Castle a few miles north of Cardiff were both made to look handsome and impressive again, and as they did old Burgess grew older and more crusty.

But of all that young Bute did whilst of age but unmarried it was the launching of the *Western Mail* that gave rise to the most comment and bitterness.

"I sincerely hope, my dear John," said Colonel Stuart, the M.P. for Cardiff, "that you'll give the matter more thought. Mr Gladstone was very much disturbed and he asked me to try and reason with you. Whatever expense has been incurred will, of course —".

"We needn't discuss that, sir," said Bute.

John Boyle, who had dined with them, asked if he might be excused to go and have a word with one of his assistants, a Welshman whose name was William Thomas Lewis.

"I'd be obliged if you would stay," said Bute.

"Very well, my lord," said Boyle.

"What you've come in such a hurry from London to prevent is almost an accomplished fact, sir," said Bute to Colonel Stuart. "And as for Mr Gladstone...well, no emissary from him could possibly influence me."

"The Prime Minister will be sorry to hear that from me, my dear John. You are young and impulsive and, in this matter, you are allowing prejudice to move you to folly. You are now a Catholic and as such you should know that the vast majority of Irish Catholics are supporters of Mr Gladstone. Here at Cardiff the few Catholics who had votes cast them for me and Mr Gladstone. Surely you know that?"

"I didn't, sir. I keep my religion out of politics."

The member for Cardiff sighed and then went on to speak more personally, pointing out that if Bute launched and maintained a Tory newspaper, to be published daily in his — the Colonel's — constituency, then it would not only place him in an embarrassing position as member for Cardiff but as kinsman as well.

"That, sir, is not my intention," said Bute. "I bear no malice towards you for what you did, as guardian and tutor-at-law, to me."

"What I did during your minority was for your own good, as your present position, excepting your change of religion, proves beyond all doubt," said the Colonel. "So I do not see how you can possibly harbour malice or even the slightest resentment. No young nobleman in this Kingdom has been better served than you, my dear John. I sincerely trust — and I'll take your word and not regard it as in the least personal. If it were then I should lose faith in you as a kinsman. For I've served you faithfully — as Boyle can tell you." He addressed himself to John Boyle. "Boyle, you took over the management of the Estate here at Cardiff and in the county in 'fifty seven, the year I was elected member for Cardiff. Now I'd like you to tell his lordship something. Since that time have you ever known me to neglect an opportunity of serving, in the House of Commons or anywhere else as opportunity presented itself, have you —".

"My dear sir," said Bute, "I grant all that. Please don't ask Mr Boyle to balance things between us. I believe that you, according to your lights, did what you thought was best for me. The fact that I, as boy and youth, didn't think so is beside the point, for you always had the whole force of the law behind all you did for me. The law was firm and so were you. The law now permits me to be firm, and — ".

"And you're determined to waste what I and Boyle and others, whose stewardship was as prudent as it was profitable, amassed for you. It may cost you anything up to a hundred thousand pounds before the thing perishes miserably. The literate minority in Cardiff and throughout Wales is far from being substantial enough to support a daily newspaper. If you have money by the hundred thousand to waste then for God's sake waste it on something less mischievous than the making and flaunting of a Tory rag! Boyle, I relied upon you to prevent his lordship from — ".

"Sir!" cried young Bute, looking most dignified, "I asked you not to call upon Mr Boyle for an opinion on this matter, a matter upon which I have already decided. And as for Mr Boyle or anyone else preventing me from acting as I think fit . . .". He smiled and shook his head. "No, sir, I have, thank God, survived the years of prevention. Another cigar, sir?"

"No, thank you," said the Colonel. "Will you be good enough to excuse me?"

"Certainly."

"Thank you. There's just one more thing. I was offered one of the lesser places in Mr Gladstone's Ministry, a place I refused in order to serve you and your Estate better; my main concern during the twelve years I have been in the House of Commons. I'll leave that with you in the hope that it may even yet influence you in the right direction. Good night, my lord."

"Good night, sir."

"Good night, Boyle."

"Good night, Colonel Stuart."

Young Bute was not in the least influenced by the words with which his kinsman revealed his devotion to Bute and the Bute Estate. The *Western Mail* was launched and Wales at last had a daily newspaper which every morning gave news of what was happening in Cardiff in particular and the world in general. If the first daily newspaper in Wales did not look like paying its way for many years to come that was nothing to worry about, for young Bute had plenty of money.

from *River out of Eden* (1951)

BERNICE RUBENS

Landsleit

The massive exodus from Eastern Europe began in earnest in the late 'seventies, and continued until the passing of the Aliens Bill in 1894. During the first wave of trickling immigration, of which Aaron Bindel was a part, the Jewish Temporary Shelter was able to cater for all the needs of the improvident immigrant. There were beds, food, clothing, holy books for prayer and help in finding employment. For many of the immigrants the Shelter was used as a stop-over haven until relatives could be traced. Aaron fell marginally into this catalogue for, though Mr Khasina was no relative, he was a known 'landsleit', or fellow-countryman. So, after a day's rest and feeding, Aaron was given enough money for his travel to Cardiff and the address of the Jewish Board of Guardians in that city. He had told the officials at the Shelter about his mother and brother. They assured him that contact would eventually be made. The Shelter was inevitably the centre and postal address for all new immigrants. They copied the address of his Cardiff sponsor and they wished him well. A Shelter official took him to the station, and instructed one of the train guards to put his passenger off at Cardiff. Aaron felt like a child and was close enough to childish tears.

The journey took many hours. The other passengers in the compartment were very talkative and they tried to include him in their conversation. He shook his head and told them in Yiddish that he didn't understand. Whereupon one of them set about giving him his first English lesson, the names of colours, features of the face and body, and all manner of emotions which they affected with charade, and in this fashion the journey passed with much enjoyment and lightened Aaron's spirits. By the time he reached Cardiff he was equipped with a minimal English vocabulary, enough to savour the sounds of the language and to accept that it would be that music that would orchestrate his future. One of the passengers offered to take him to Mr Khasina's address. He himself, he mimed, lived in the neighbourhood. It was dark when they arrived in Cardiff and Aaron feared that it might be too late to make such an unexpected call. But his companion indicated that he need not worry and he urged him along the narrow streets checking the numbers on the doors against the piece of paper in Aaron's hand. At last they reached Khasina's dwelling. Aaron bade farewell to his companion, thanking him. Then he pulled the bell at the side of the door. He listened as the echo died away but he heard no footsteps towards the door. He wouldn't ring again, he decided. He would wait a while, then go away with a certain relief. He would somehow find his way to the Board of Guardians. He was about to turn from the door when it opened. A man stood there, slippered, Aaron noted, which accounted for the silence of his approach. His father would have been the man's age, Aaron thought, and for that reason, immediately resented him, so he gave his name coldly and asked for Pavel Khasina. The man smiled and turned his head indoors.

"Pavel," he shouted. "A 'landsleit'."

Shortly afterwards Pavel himself appeared at the door and scrutinised the caller. After a while he cried out, "Odessa. The tavern. The widow. Two sons. Come in, my friend. You took my advice."

The welcome was lavish. They led him through the front room which Aaron could discern as a shop of sorts, but it was dark and it was difficult to decipher what was sold. At the back of the shop were the living-quarters, not unlike the lay-out, Aaron thought, of Grandpa Jakob's tavern. And the kitchen was similar too, where all the living took place, the cooking and the eating, and there was even a small truckle-bed in the corner.

"For you," Pavel Khasina said, and he took Aaron's bags and put them on the bed. Then he introduced his sister, Hinda, his brother-in-law, Max, the slippered one who had opened the door, and two or three friends, 'Landsleit' too, Khasina explained. And just like the tavern, the samovar stood in the centre of the table.

All were eager for news of home. They knew no one in common, no friends, no relatives, but that was not where their interest lay. Their nostalgia was for the land, the language, even the cruelty; they needed to hear about it, to reminisce each chapter of their own survival and to celebrate the fact that they were now beyond its reach. But they kept silent. They wanted him fed and fortified. Then, when he was sated, they could sniff out the land on him, that land which had borne and bred them, hated and abused them, and in which they had left their dead. Aaron ate in a watchful silence and when he had done, Pavel poured wine for them all, and they drank a toast to his welcome.

Then "What news of home?" one of them asked, giving Aaron an opening and making it as general as possible. But Aaron had only his own personal story to tell, but that was general enough, for it could have happened to any of them. He told it from the beginning, back-tracking occasionally when questions were asked which called for clarification from the past. So that when the long recital was over, he had told them not only his own tale, but that of his father's and Grandpa Jakob's as well. During the telling, they nodded with signs of recognition because many of the events had coloured their own lives too. They drank another glass of wine together, and then they spent much time speculating on what could have happened to Zelda and Leon. Their prognoses varied, but fundamentally they were all the same. "Soon you will all be together again," they said.

The phrase had a familiar ring. From the stories Grandpa Jakob had told him, it was with exactly those words that he had bade farewell to the milk-brothers. Had not the gentle Leon used that phrase too, he after whom his brother was named? It was that hope and conviction of family reunion that Leon had shouted from the dock before his one-way Siberian journey. And finally his own father had said it, as he kissed them and sent them off to Zemach's tavern to prepare for his eighty-fifth birthday. "Soon we shall all be together again," he had said. Aaron did not like that phrase, and he wished that those around the table had not voiced it. "Please God," he whispered. Perhaps if he appended a prayer, it might come true.

The following morning, Aaron was awoken by the bustle in the kitchen. Hinda was making breakfast for the family. Two little girls materialised; they had obviously been in bed when Aaron had arrived. They stared at the new-comer on the cot, then turned away, giggling. Aaron rose and dressed quickly. Soon Max came to the table and Pavel. Aaron was invited to sit between the children who were chattering freely in English. Pavel explained that in front of the children only English was spoken. The children were their teachers and would be Aaron's teachers too. So for Aaron it was a silent meal until the children left for school. Then it was Yiddish again around the table with plans for Aaron's future. His first move, they suggested, and on that very day, was to go to the Jewish Board of Guardians and register his immigrant status. They would help him with money until he could find work. His lodgings on the kitchen bed would be free, they assured him, until he found his feet. The Board held classes for English too. It would be somewhere for him to go during the day. As to the prospect of work, Pavel offered to train him in the job that he did himself. Pavel was a credit draper. This was a trade most favoured by those immigrants who did not have a particular skill. Its great advantage was that it required little initial capital and even that could be credited. The trade itself was concerned with the sale of clothing to lower income groups at the minimum payment of a shilling a week, and the main hunting-ground for such clientèle was the Welsh mining valleys. The tally man would buy his goods on credit from the wholesale merchants, then make the rounds of his customers. The profit margin was narrow, the work-hours long and arduous, but it already provided Pavel with a living, as it did many of his 'landsleit'. Some of them, after a year or two, had bought their own houses, and some, like Max, had used the profits to set up a shop of their own.

Max's shop was sited on the long busy thoroughfare that led to the docks. The docks at Cardiff were a harbour for cargo from all over the world and the wagons of imported grain would pass the out-going coal-wagons as they trundled to and from the dock-side. The area was rich in passing trade. Many of the early immigrants set up small businesses there, catering for the needs of sailors and ship personnel. Max's shop sold men's clothing and luggage, and wooden chests and tin trunks stood on the forefront. Tailoring establishments were sandwiched between ale-houses and brothels. At first sight the area could have been any port in the world. Only the line of coal-wagons shuttling down Bute Street gave a clue to its Welsh location.

It was into this confusing and alien thoroughfare that Aaron was launched, on his first morning, a carefully drawn map in his hand, to make his way to the Jewish Board of Guardians. As he walked he worried about Zelda and Leon and wondered what had become of them. Such thoughts always led to the image of some calamity that had befallen. Perhaps he should go back to Hamburg. But, even if he had the money to get there, where and how would he start looking? Perhaps the Jewish Board had a representative there. He quickened his pace, and from time to time, he checked on the map in his hand. He was so concerned about his family's welfare, that he had little curiosity about his strange surroundings. He would have felt guilty to find a possible pleasure in their novelty. He considered that all his energies must be channelled into the search for his mother and brother.

In time he reached the offices of the Board where a member, noting his immigrant garb and confusion, spoke to him in Yiddish and welcomed him. Aaron sat down on the chair that was offered him but he declined a glass of lemon tea. He was anxious to appraise the official of the loss of his family, to seek help in finding them. The official was baffled by the story.

But he would make enquiries, he promised, taking their names and particulars. He then concerned himself with Aaron's personal financial needs and gave him the address of a school where every evening he could attend classes in the English language. Aaron left the officers of the Board, his spirits lightened. Now someone else, someone in authority, would share with him the responsibility, if not the concern, for finding his family.

That evening he attended his first English lesson. There were a dozen or so pupils and most of them were older than Aaron. A new-comer was assured of welcome because the smell of home still lingered on his gaberdine, and although most of them, as it turned out, hailed from Poland, their mother-tongue was common, and all had fled from like oppression. One of the group, the youngest, was a girl who introduced herself as Rachel and who had recently arrived from Lodz. She offered Aaron a seat on the bench beside her. It was a rule in the class that once a lesson had begun no Yiddish was to be spoken, so for Aaron it was a silent hour. But he was able to learn a little and to begin to draw the letters of a strange alphabet. When the lesson was finished, he found himself walking into the street with Rachel at his side. Out of politeness he offered to see her to her home, an offer which she accepted on condition that they spoke no Yiddish on their way. So once again Aaron was driven to silence. And so it was, night after night, after the English lesson, until in time, as the weeks passed, he was able to talk to her, and to share with her his cares and occasional hopes. And with words now between them, he began to grow fond of her.

from *Brothers* (1983)

ALEXANDER CORDELL

A Little Terraced House

It never rains but it pours, and Mr Franklin and my mother were married in St Paul's Catholic Church in the summer of 1887, with my Uncle Ocker, still single (I was scared to death for Carrie) and holding the ring. There was a lot of sniffing and sobbing and Aunt Emily nearly fainting off, and half the population of Newtown were there to give happy congratulations, and me tied up in my new Sunday suit with my starched collar killing me.

Very alcoholic it all was, with the customers turning out of the taverns and a musical contingent from the Harp of Old Ireland present with drums and Irish bagpipes and Bridie Corrigan's cart and donkey bringing up the rear for those who couldn't travel.

Mind you, my family was a cut above all this; we always kept to ourselves, but you couldn't stop the guests arriving; the men in polished bowlers and the women done up in grape-assembly hats. Weddings, and particularly funerals, were always well attended in Newtown, but it's a scandal, said my gran, that a decent couple couldn't get married in Irishtown without Crockherbtown riff-raff taking part.

Very pretty my mother looked on the day she married Frank Franklin, and I saw her glance towards the railway shunting yard on her way home, for it was in there that my father had been run over.

It is strange to me that God takes two people and joins them together in body and spirit . . .then takes one away and cuts him in half. I knew what Ma was thinking; like me, her mind was up by Plot F576 in Cathays cemetery. Although I never knew my father, Cornelius Driscoll, he was striding in my heart.

Perhaps Frank Franklin knew of this? But he guessed enough, I think, to take us out of Twelve Ellen Street and move us into Eleven Herbert, at the top of Bute West dock. What is there, I wonder, about the rooms of a little terraced house that leans shoulder to shoulder with its friends to keep out the wind?

Gran and Aunty Emily stayed on, of course, for Emily was courting strong with a fella now, and soon, said Carrie, the place would be filled with little screechin' childer.

With Gran down at Cardiff market and Emily in the shop, I walked around the rooms after the family had gone: here the stair that creaks, there the same old spider on the landing that Ma couldn't reach; here the chair where my gran sits, there the bed where I once slept with Carrie.

When you poked the fire the grate smiled its redness, one tooth missing in front; dolefully, the tin bath hangs on the wall out the back, speckled with tears at being out all night — don't forget to bring it, Driscoll, that's your job, they said. The kitchen smelled of food and Gran's bags of lavender stitched into her skirts; my father's pipe rack was on the wall, forgotten, so I prised it off and put it in my pocket. The trouble with Twelve Ellen Street was the rent — six shillings a week, enough to break us.

The new house in Herbert Street was even more; God help us, I thought, for my new father was only a dock labourer on thirteen shillings, and that was if he didn't get 'blobbed' — laid off.

With the tin bath on my back I went around to Herbert Street, and there the family was moving in: one there was a very old friend, Minnie Looney.

"A little wedding present from Newtown," said little Minnie who was married to Potty Poole, living up in Adamsdown, and she dropped the shillings into my mother's hands.

"Oh no, Min, they can't afford it!" protested Ma.

"Please take it, Liz — the least we can do, being Irish."

Frank Franklin said: "Thank you, Miss Looney," and bowed to her.

Five feet up and drooping in her old man's suit, Miss Looney smiled her rhubarb smile: bow tie, bowler, big square boots, with a toe sticking out: married these forty years to Potty, the seamstress, and though folks said they weren't a full pound, Potty had a wedding-ring to prove it: love is a very funny thing, said Carrie, it turns folks inside out; when Newtown dies the soul will move out of Cardiff. . . .

From the time I was five years old I helped my mother sell fish up and down the streets of Newtown. Up at the crack of dawn, the pair of us, for at eight o'clock Ma had to start her potato bundling in the ships coming into England Wharf.

"Come on, look lively!"

Scarfed and shawled against the sea wind we'd go with our old pram to meet the Neale and West trawlers coming in from Cardiff Bay; this was long before little Tommy Letton sold fish from his barrow down Bute. And there, already waiting at the gutting tables, were the fish-wives of Newtown and Adamsdown, and you've never heard such a babble since they found Disraeli in bed with a widow at the Cow and Snuffers, said Carrie. With blood-red hands they'd slit and chop the herring, plopping the entrails into crimson buckets, and the language coming up from those tables was enough to take the shine off cassocks.

"Wait here, Driscoll," my mother would say, "it's cold up there on the dock," but I knew it was only because of the swearing women. Shivering, I'd wait till she came back with the pram loaded with herring, cod, mullet and skate — mackerel when in season.

By this time Newtown was awake; doors opening, dust being broomed out, lights going on in kitchen windows, babies being breasted or bottled, old men with dangling braces mooching down the garden, cats being booted, grans and granchers blowing at tea.

"Fresh fish! Herrings and dabs, mullet and cod!"

There were no ladies around when my mother was the fishmonger. She bawled her wares like a man with my piping treble coming up in between: this was after my father died and before Frank Franklin came, of course. Through the cracked window of One Ellen Street I can see Billy O'Hara as we turn the corner for home. Off his food, so his mam says, since Carrie gave him the shove. Now, frowsed with sleep, he droops, scratching. Now he's at his door.

"Is Carys back from London, Mrs Driscoll?"

Plaintive, he begs, all two yards of him, and as far as I knew she'd never seen the skies over London.

"Carrie must speak for herself, Billy O'Hara," replied my mother.

His trews slip down and he hauls them up, shivering in the frost. "Will ye put a word in for me, ma'am? I'm off the blob, ye know — working with your Flurrie on Atlantic Wharf, so I am . . .".

"Aw, come on, O'Hara, where's the man in you?"

"Fresh from the bay," I shouted, giving him a wink. "Away wi' you, mun, she's having 'em two at a time, ye haven't a chance."

Which was true; December thought it was June when Carrie got going. The pram grinds on down to Number Twelve, and my mother said:

"That's no way to talk, Driscoll; remember it."

"Yes, Ma."

"And no way for a man to behave — or Carys either," and her lips were pursed red as if she'd been eating cherries.

I chanced a glance at her; I never heard her speak that way about Carrie, and she added: "When folks come home after midnight, the Devil's parading his broom. She must think we've been raised in Kibby's

Asylum." Which surprised me more. I was under the impression Carrie didn't give a damn for fellas.

Mind, there was a bit of talk about Carrie around then, who was rising sixteen and learning what day it was, said Gran. And some of the brightness had gone out of the kitchen, which can come pretty dull when folks fall out. Old Mrs Cumber who lived on ale and gossip, said she'd raise her garters for a wink over a hedge, but I didn't know what she meant.

You could take lumps out of the silence some nights, when Carrie did herself up for prancing out; when you live with decent people ye keep yourself decent, said my mother.

And the chaps kept coming, hanging on the walls outside like string beans and things were cool within.

I hate the house when it is at odds with itself and folks go to bed without kissing goodnight. And I would lie up there in the belly of the bed with Mary Ann snoring one side of me and Carrie saying her prayers on the other.

"Please God, don't let me have a baby," she was whispering. "Please God, don't let me have a baby."

I could never get the hang of that, for you can't have a baby until you're married, according to Boyo, my mate. And you canna get up to any tricks at all, said he, until you're twenty-one.

from *Peerless Jim* (1984)

HOWARD SPRING

Street Boys

When you told a boy you'd meet him at Joe Andrew's Stone, he knew well enough what you meant; for to us the Stone was a landmark as geographically important as the Cape or the Horn to more distant wanderers.

Our street was short, but nevertheless it was cut in two by another street that ran across it. Standing at the cross-road, looking to one end of our street and then to the other, you would see little to choose. The houses were identical. Each one of them contained a sitting-room, a kitchen and a scullery downstairs, a stairway that ran up between walls with no banister or rail, and two bedrooms.

At each end of the street you would see a high wall, closing the uninspiring view, so that whether, coming into the street from the cross-road, you turned right or left, you were in a dead end.

Nothing to choose then, looking from the cross-road. Yet in our end of the street the other end was always spoken of as The Other End. We understood, yet knew not why we understood, that The Other End was nefarious and evil. "Don't go down The Other End" my mother would say; and I remember as one of the queer facts of childhood that, for all the years I lived in the street, not once did I go down The Other End.

Joe Andrew's public house stood at the intersection of the roads; and in a corner of the wall was the tar-blackened buttress that was Joe Andrew's Stone. The fathers of the street met in Joe Andrew's bright bar; the boys consorted each night at the Stone.

Thence we ranged on our simple pleasures. It was unfortunate for Mr Hann that every time the door of his corner shop was opened a bell rang. He would come from the parlour behind the shop, rubbing his hands in his apron in expectation of some such petty sale as his miserable stock permitted, and find a grinning row of young fiends chanting:

"Hann, Hann,
Catch us if you can."

He would fling up the flap of the counter and plunge spasmodically towards us, only to find that his quarry had disappeared into the dark lane

27

that ran behind our street with the electric speed of a shoal of minnows among whom a stone had been dropped.

But Hann was a tactician ever alert to devise new methods of outwitting his tormentors. His first essay at counter-measures was a long cane, concealed behind the row of glass jars that shone with all the delectable and deceptive colours of cheap confectionery. Emerging from the parlour one night, he feigned a dull stupidity as he stared at ten dancing impudent eyes set in five impertinent faces; then with lightning speed grabbed the cane, threw his body across the counter, and slashed.

It taught us caution; we hovered nearer the door next night, more swiftly poised for flight. Alas! that it did not suggest something of the cunning of our enemy. For not long after that, no sooner did the bell ring and we stand there gazing with unholy rapture at the lighted panes of the parlour door, than Hann leapt from concealment behind a parapet of sacks loaded to their chins with split peas and potatoes; and there for the first time in our experience was the baited bear among the terriers. He seized me in a grip of iron, bent me in one masterly stroke across his knee, and with a flat brush, designed for the sweeping of carpets but alas! not ill-adapted to more lethal ends, proceeded to demonstrate the inadequacy of my trousers.

Perhaps it was this revelation of Hann's readiness to meet enterprise with craft that turned our thoughts for much of that winter to the safer delights of Rap-tap-ginger. A game simple enough, God knows, consisting, in its crude and inartistic form, of merely banging on the neighbours' knockers and crying Rap-tap-ginger as you fled from the wrath to come.

It was Joe Blain, ever an alert and enterprising mind, who raised this horse-play to the status of an eerie art. A neighbouring street was well designed to meet the needs of the case, for the houses on one side of the street were flat to the pavement, while on the other side were niggardly yards of soured earth where privets pushed an untidy growth against the rails.

A piece of blackened string was fastened to a knocker, the string was carried to our ambush behind the privets, and a pull set the knocker at work. Again and again some wretched householder was drawn from the peace and comfort of his fireside; and we, trembling behind the privets, savoured to the full a deep conviction that that householder must sooner or later attribute the knockings to a ghostly agency.

Running Round the Block was another joy of winter nights, the competitors starting from the same point and running in opposite directions. We had paced the track and marked with white chalk the halfway point; and what horror it was to find that your opponent was past the point — five, ten or fifteen yards — before you reached it! How, then, your heart pumped, and you urged your feet, cased in heavy hob-nailed boots, to a tremendous endeavour! Awful those moments of isolation, not seeing your flying foe, but knowing that not far away he, too, was panting his young heart out, bent on adding insolence to victory by running out to meet you!

But perhaps our greatest joy was that which depended on awful and grisly provision. Not far away was the slaughter-house, to which, in defiance of all rules and orders, we would often creep, drawn by the repulsion of its dreadful sights and sounds and smells. In our street there lived a man who gained his living in that shambles, and we would waylay his homeward march and beg the boon of a pig's bladder.

He was an apparition from Hell, a little shambling man with a squint, whose clothes and hands were always imbrued with blood. I could never see him without a shudder; but he was kind enough, and always our petition would be granted. Taking a bloody mess from his pocket, he would throw it to us, and there were, fortunately, boys who, with no qualms at all, would blow it up; and then the game would be on.

Playing football with a pig's bladder, enclosed in no leather case, is an exercise fit for fairies, and goodness knows there were no fairies among us. The game soon ended either with the bursting of the ball or with a shrill cry of "Creeping Jesus!"

I do not know why the sergeant of police had received that name, though the adjective was appropriate. One moment he was not; and the next, lo! in all his panoply he was materialising in the misty winter night. I have at this distance of time no difficulty in supposing that he was a simple and human being; but then his mere appearance convinced us all of unimaginable guilt, and, taking to our heels, we would run till he was out of sight, and then steal home by the darkest and most devious ways. No citizen as law-abiding as myself has fled the officers of the law through so many terror-stricken miles.

Terror is a dreadful companion once you have admitted him to your heart. From the start, there was terror for me in our street. The Other End held terrors unguessed. The women sitting on their doorsteps in the hot summer nights might have been hags from Hell; the men, with their cruelly-buckled leather belts, lounging towards Joe Andrew's pub, looked fierce and inimical; and old Feany who lived opposite to us, and set out every morning with a great basket of crockery on his head to cry his wares about the streets, seemed always to me a presence to be peculiarly dreaded. Never once in my young life did I speak a word to old Feany, or he to me; yet it would not have surprised me had he suddenly swooped upon me and subjected me to diabolic torture.

And this is how the Terror came to me. I do not know how old I was when we went to the street, but I must have been five or six. We shifted, as poor people do, with the aid of a handcart. My father carted such furniture as there was from the old house to the new one in a series of journeys, and on one of these journeys he took me and my brother with him. He took us into the kitchen, and sat us side by side on his old wooden arm-chair. Then he left us, and went away for another cartload.

It was wintertime, and the night was coming on. We were alone in that strange dark house. A glimmer of fire burned in the grate on our right: in front of us was an uncurtained window, giving upon blackness. The stairs in that house always creaked. They creaked of their own accord without anyone setting foot upon them. They creaked that night. We sat there, two babes in the wood of Terror, clutching one another, speaking no word, looking at the dark window and listening to the stairs creaking.

Then through the night there boomed suddenly the sound of a great drum beating. Loud voices were upraised singing "The Lamb, the Lamb, the bleeding Lamb," and upon them all burst a greater voice that shrieked through the night "The Blood!"

Still we spoke no word. We sat and trembled in that forlorn and empty house, and listened to the voice crying "The Blood!"

We soon got to know it as a regular performance: that arrival of the Salvation Army outside Joe Andrew's pub, the rush from the bar of Mrs Murphy, the street's most notorious drunkard. The singing of the hymns converted her every time she heard them; crying upon the Blood she would rush forth, join the singers, march with them to their barracks, and be at Joe's again the next night.

So the Terror came to the street. Always to me the house in some sort was haunted. Sleepless, I would listen to the stairs creaking below me; to the thudding of the drum, to the cries upon the Blood; and to these were added now and then the shrieks of beaten women, the commotion of the arriving police; and then, when everything else was quiet, again the stairs would creak as though impalpable beings had weight and were ascending and descending.
from *Heaven Lies About Us* (1939)

R.T. JENKINS

A Merry and Delightful Place

The first time I saw the city of Cardiff was on Whitsun holiday in 1905, when I went there with one of my fellow-teachers. Pleasure was not our only purpose; we were on important business, namely the purchase of a new horn for the gramophone that we looked after in the lodgings — the one we had was inadequate; that is to say, probably, it didn't make enough noise to please us! . . .
I fell in love with Cardiff immediately, a love that has never grown cold. Not that I remember exactly what I saw in 1905, apart from a visit to Llandaff Cathedral on Sunday morning. But I liked the town very much — the city, rather, because it had just been promoted to that status; proof of this was the fact that Castle Road had been re-christened City Road — the shop where we bought the gramophone horn was there. A city much smaller than the Cardiff of today. St Mary Street was the main street in 1905; there was a shabby, unfinished look to Queen Street, which by now is the city's main thoroughfare. Duke Street a narrow lane whose length the traffic could not negotiate; Cathays Park little more than the beginnings of the cluster of grand buildings which are the city's source of pride today. The suburbs less extensive, and at the same time more separate, not in one solid block as they are today. I had a colleague in Cardiff School, who wasn't much older than I, and he could remember the fields which by 1914 had been covered by rows of houses between Newport Road (note Newport Road — not Street) and Roath Park. Yes, Cardiff in 1905 was swimming *on* the tide, with the world (so it seemed) at its feet. I saw with my own eyes street after street changing from 'residential' to 'business' — shops and offices creeping from the corner of City Road up Newport Road as far as Broadway and beyond; Wellfield Road following the example of Albany Road by plastering shop-fronts on the faces of private houses; the slopes of Pen-y-lan turning into shelves of streets; Cyncoed and Rhydypennau, where the wife and I rambled 'in the country' on Sunday afternoons, being filled with houses; the Three Arches lane becoming a street, and so on — the same, too, down Canton and Ely way and even distant Rhiwbina — the village where I lived from 1920 to 1930, completely surrounded by 1940 with bricks and mortar. Nevertheless, I saw this tide turning, too; but now the future of Cardiff is very

insecure. I shall hardly see grass ever growing between the stones of its pavements; yet it is on the turn, I fear now, because the coal-pits were the foundation of Cardiff's success; the ships carrying the coal to the four corners of the Earth; the crowds swarming down from the valleys to the city's shops and delights on a Thursday or Saturday afternoon; the small industries and the businesses catering for the needs or showing off of its clerks and shoppers, and which filled the pockets of its proud and prosperous traders. St Mary Street on Saturday morning was proverbial for the handsome appearance and the beauty of the expensive clothes of the daughters of the town's dignitaries. But it was the little collier in Tonypandy or Cwmaman, in the end, who had created all this splendour and beauty; and when the moth and rust began to pollute the collier, the fine flowers of Cardiff began to wither. . . .

Yet in 1905, and come to that in 1917, there was no sign of this. I, and my wife with me, was many a time in Cardiff bent on pleasure. We remember that it was there we both saw an opera for the first time — that was *Tanhäuser*. I remember buying in the Spring of 1917, from a stall upstairs in the Market, a brand-new and perfectly clean copy of *Y Bardd Cwsc* in John Morris-Jones's edition, for a shilling — at a time when booksellers were asking thirty shillings for it. Yes, Cardiff was a merry and delightful place.

translated by Meic Stephens from *Edrych yn Ôl* (1968)

TOM DAVIES

The Big Game

At Cardiff General Station the group spilled out of the train, a flying wedge that went scything through the singing passions and sizzling shunts of the crowd assembled from all over the country for the big game. Bedragoned flags fluttered above the heads of the copper-ladlers, colliers, tin-platers, seamen, clerks and shippers. Many were carrying fat leeks with some, flush out of leeks, waving strings of onions about since onions, at least, had the same violent smell, redolent of a dead and dying enemy.

The cavernous gloomy bars — built by Brains Brewery as a tribute to a nation's insatiable and monumental thirst — were as packed as sardines in tins, the air a smoke-laden, beer-scented fug as overflowing pints slopped this way and that — sometimes even down throats. Outside the bars there was slightly more air to breathe in Queen Street and St Mary's Street, where singing Welshmen, celebrating in advance, swung, ape-like, on lamp posts as ragged urchins begged for pennies, sold matches or stood around the glowing chestnut braziers on each corner to keep warm. Men were wading across the River Taff in the hope of climbing into the Arms Park without paying. Policemen stayed well back as drunks ricocheted along the cobbles of Quay Street.

The Penclawdd flying wedge flew into The Albert where Marnie, first to the bar, began passing back a frothing series of pints of the famous dark. In the far corner they then got down to some serious drinking and returned yet again to The Discussion:

"That Gwyn Nicholls could play fifteen Englishers all on his own, he could. You know, I've got a real fancy we're up for the Triple Crown this year. The All Blacks next season, too. I'm not at all sure we're up to them."

"'Course we are, mun — if only we can get rid of that . . .".

When kick-off time approached Michael was three parts gone as they formed yet another flying wedge straight to the ground, where they each paid a shilling at the wooden barrier and shouldered their way into the ground itself.

Michael knew of nothing quite like those early moments when he stood with his countrymen in this enormous theatre where a dramatic people were preparing to set up a series of genuine and passionate responses to a great struggle. Huge spasms of emotion rolled around and around the crowds; hymns and arias burst out from different sections of the bob bank, duelling with one another under stands which were themselves shaking with the steady thunder of stamping, impatient feet.

The Penclawdd lads were so off their chumps with excitement they could barely speak. Even a fully qualified atheist like Michael could see, as he stood there, feeling this tribal electricity pulsing through his blood, how close rugby was to the chapel at the heart of the Welsh revelation; how both pulpit and goal post formed a focus for the same profound expressions of a tribe's view of itself as following a path of crusading fire.

Antagonistic though he was to the work of Evan Roberts he saw that the chapel's insights into the freedom of poverty and the rugby world's absolute insistence on amateurism reflected the same purity of values. The chapel talk of brotherhood and equality before the cross, and Welsh rugby's classlessness and sacrifice of the solo dash for team effort, voiced the same instinct for democracy. When forty thousand choristers in this ground, the largest massed choir in the world, lifted their voices — as they were doing now — and sang William Williams' 'Guide Me O Thou Great Jehovah' it was a massed heartfelt prayer that they might all be fed with the bread of heaven: an incredible number of points. . . .

When kick-off time came some of the Penclawdd boys felt so anxious they set about relieving themselves, with Michael and others dancing around trying to avoid getting their trousers wet and warm. Well, Michael thought, that's one thing they don't do in the chapel.

Seagulls wheeled up high in the dull cloudy sky, their excellent view matched only by that of the Press and selectors who sat on a trestle table just next to the touch-line. The National Anthem was sung, the Welsh captain won the toss — the Lord really *was* looking on Wales with favour that winter — the whistle blew and for the next hour and twenty minutes the scarlet warriors of Wales put the white-shirted Sassenachs of England through the mangle, slow.

Fantastic, it was. All the Penclawdd boys just kept weeping and laughing with an almost certifiable dementia. Michael was transported straight to heaven; such feelings of jubilation sweeping up and down his body his rigor mortis didn't have a hope of attacking him.

Right from the kick-off the Welsh set up base camp on the English twenty-five and the giant Welsh forwards mauled and spoiled every English move. Fearless in the rucks, they were, and ready to castrate bulls with their teeth in the scrums. Steadier and tighter than a Roman

34

phalanx the Welsh forwards kept driving forward, the steam rising off their backs as they sent out a steady flow of clean passes to the Welsh backs, who romped this way and that, faster and nippier than greyhounds with boiling hormones.

The chief Welsh executioners were the two outside halves — Richard Owen and Richard Jones, the legendary Dancing Dicks — who sliced and chopped the English defence into tiny diced cubes, dashing one way and another with now-you-see-now-you-don't runs, catching the ball with either hand or even their shoulder blades, leaving the English leaden-footed, heartbroken and very sorry indeed that they had ever given up hockey and so much as seen a rugby ball in the first place.

Throughout the game Michael and the boys kept doing little jigs of joy and hugging one another as the sweet carnage continued. Michael was so overcome by one try he kissed Howard Morgan hard on the lips — making Howard the first man he had ever kissed with any real passion. Joy affected people in different ways; Marnie just kept vomiting, noisy, while others sang until their vocal cords were no better than a battered bit of string. "Feeeeeeeeed me 'til I waaaaaaant no more."

Even on the odd occasions when the English got the ball they could do nothing with it, still less penetrate the Welsh defence since the selectors had sensibly got rid of that Llanelli rubbish, Jack Strand-Jones, at full-back and brought in George Davies from Cardiff in his place. Davies had the presence and effect of a brick wall, converting two of the Welsh tries as well. Other scorers were Teddy Morgan, Rhys Gabe, Harry Watkins, Arthur Harding and Richard 'Dancing Dick' Jones, who gave their nation tries which still live and burn in the Welsh memory like some fearsome sin.

Come the final whistle the English captain went up to the Welsh goal line to see what it looked like.

The final score was Wales twenty-five, England nil and, after the last whistle, as huge cataracts of relieved urine cascaded down out of the stands, the exhilaration was even more unconfined and buoyant than on that momentous day when they relieved Mafeking. Joy poured out of the ground, mounted the backs of telegram wires, slapped itself on handbills and posters, was carried by cart and by bicycle, was shouted and echoed down valleys until it all came together in a great tidal wave which rolled straight across Wales until it collapsed into the Atlantic.

Michael was carried in a rolling, singing crush out of the ground, across the road and swept into the corner of a bar in the Queen's Vaults. Hoarse and very thirsty, everyone kept hugging one another and drinking any pint or whisky that seemed to be standing around available, as if some great mythic river of alcohol had burst over their heads, sudden. Some stood discussing and analysing the moves of the game in the lilting accents of West Wales or the hard, harsh vowels of Cardiff, others were singing 'Sospan Fach', 'Bill Bailey' and 'Boys of the Old Brigade' — one song after another or even, if you like, all at the same time. If they could not remember the words and were drifting, comatose, towards the floor they would always sing soft into their beer: "Feeeeeeeeeed me 'til I waaaaaaaant no more."

Many songs — and even more drinks — later everything had gone hazy and Michael was reasonably sure that there was fighting going on all around him. He had no objection to that except that someone — a Sassenach probably . . . tried to steal his drink in the fray. Right out of his hand! He punched someone or something, went rolling one way with a massive explosion of pain in his left ear, before reeling backwards retreating from yet another explosion in his nose.

Next thing he knew, there were three men kicking him with one sitting on his chest. Hah now, he thought to himself, quiet. Hah now, I've got them all where I want them.

All around him he heard the eruptions of tumbling tables and the bright shattering of breaking glass. Suddenly, over the other side of the bar, he spotted what appeared to be a row of Cardiff policemen, individuals famous throughout the ports of the world for their wonderful sense of humour and loving tenderness.

Michael came around some four hours later, in a cell in Cardiff police station. Others were lying around, bleeding and groaning: some were still discussing the game with one another through the bars.

He tried to move but could not; his rigor mortis — or something even deadlier — had got him down his side. "I've got this girl who keeps making bits of me go dead," he told a man slumped in the corner of the cell. "Ever heard of anything like that, have you?"

There was a distant scream of someone being tenderized by a policeman's truncheon. The man in the corner of the cell looked up, his eyes bruised black and nose still running red like a pair of taps. "My Mam is going to make bits of me go dead when she finds out about this," he wailed. "My Mam will bloody kill me for this."

Michael groaned deep in his pain again. Those parts of his body that were not giving him pain were still drunk. "One minute it's that leg, then it's this leg. My back will be going soon and I'm that fed up with it all I wish they'd keep me in here forever. How'd I get in here anyway?"

"Anyone in here know the score?"

"Twenty-five bloody points to bloody nil that's what the score was."

"And let's face it, boys," said a tousle-haired lad in the cell opposite when the cheering had stopped. "Let's face it now. England were bloody lucky to get the nil!"

from *One Winter of the Holy Spirit* (1985)

ERIC LINKLATER

A Temporary Habitation

The camaraderie of the sea brought Robert Linklater and Elizabeth Young together again, but when they decided on marriage they were faced with two decisions, both necessary, that neither relished. My father's last command in sail was a big, four-masted barque called *Celticburn*, and from her broad quarterdeck he had to transfer himself to a steamship's bridge. That was a transition which he and my grandfather, and all right-thinking men of their sort, regarded as a fearful degradation, but which young men could not avoid because sailing ships were no longer profitable, and steamships offered them the only livelihood for which they had been taught. The new firm by which Robert was employed owned ships that sailed from Bristol Channel ports — from Cardiff or Avonmouth — to East Africa and South Africa by way of the Mediterranean; and Elizabeth Young would have to leave the little town on the Clyde in which, when she was not at sea, she had spent her early years. She bitterly resented the migration, and her resentment had a curious effect on my childhood: I was led to believe that we were living in exile.

My mother had no drop of Scots blood in her — her father was Swedish, her mother English — but she was a woman of fierce and determined character who had arbitrarily decided that she was Scotch; and Scotch she remained when she went to live in South Wales.

I was born in Penarth, of which I have no memory, for while I was still an infant — or perhaps a little older — we removed to a new, protruding limb of the city of Cardiff. The limb was a benign and well-gardened series of public parks which modest rows of small houses accompanied. I have never returned to Cardiff since we left it in 1912 or 1913, but now, when town-planning is so highly regarded, I am inclined to think that, sixty years ago, it must have been in the vanguard of municipal progress. I was very happy there, despite my mother's insistence that our habitation was no more permanent than a gipsy's camp; but I was happier still when she took us to Orkney for long summer holidays. Of them I shall have more to say later. At the moment my topic is Cardiff.

Its principal pleasures, as my memory retains them, were bicycles, small rowing boats, a series of plump, dark-haired little girls — most of them, I think, called Gwynneth — and food. Of food, that grave and splendid topic, I shall defer discussion. The boats were for hire on a large lake in one of the parks, and from an early age I had a season-ticket that let me take useful exercise and enjoy the unfailing pleasure of plank-thin proximity to water. The bicycles and the plump little girls were closely associated, and there were picnic parties as far afield as Caerphilly.

My education had its beginning — an unhelpful beginning — in a dames' school conducted by two tiny, fragile grey-complexioned old ladies called the Misses Jennings, whose young assistant — a rosy, bouncing, pretty girl to whom I was perversely attached — clouded for many years my apprehension of arithmetic by a system of instruction which — for me, at any rate — invested mere integers with the incomprehensibility of Egyptian hieroglyphs before discovery of the Rosetta Stone. I doted on my rosy teacher, but quailed before the sinister nonsense of the little white sums she chalked on her blackboard.

Some time later I was entered at the curious nucleus of a school which has since become much respected as the Cardiff High School. It was then housed, in part, in temporary hutments of a sort which became familiar in times of war; and was known, without much appreciation of the emotional significance of names, as the Cardiff Intermediate School for Boys. We wore, on striped caps, badges which carried those unimpressive initials C.I.S.B. and twice or three times a week we played association football, hockey, or cricket. More freely, and without supervision, we also put on padded gloves to play fives in concrete courts which, in a building-programme, had been given priority over permanent classrooms.

I remember few of the boys who were my companions, but I can recall, very clearly, the appearance and habit of several of the masters. There was a splendid man, who taught Classics, called Mr Brace or Mr Bryce. He was an atheist who stood defiantly erect during morning prayers ostentatiously despising their unwarranted appeal. He had two sons, as gaunt and seemingly as under-nourished as their father; and he used to say that no one could call himself a gentleman who had no knowledge of Homer's Greek. There was Todger Evans, excessively Welsh, with a strange domestic smell, of whom I was very fond. There were one or two rank adventurers, flashy men who obviously were taking a job between jobs, to provide a living while they looked for something better. There was a delightful man — called, I think, Grieg — who took some of us to see Glamorgan play Gloucestershire at cricket and told us to watch, with close attention, everything that Gilbert Jessop did. "Not only while he's batting! Anyone can enjoy Jessop's batting. He's got a wonderful eye, and scores very quickly. But watch him while he's fielding, and then you'll see the real artist that's in him." And there was a master of a very different sort, a little, pursy, ill-tempered teacher of elementary science whom I met again, several years later, in improbable circumstances that I shall describe with much pleasure in a later chapter.

A contributory factor in my mother's aversion to Cardiff was David Lloyd George and the fact that he, like her neighbours, was Welsh. In the early years of this century there were many shipping companies whose mushroom enrichment owed something to gross neglect of the comfort and safety of their ships and ships' companies; and Lloyd George, as President of the Board of Trade, contributed to the dangers of seafaring by his decision to raise the Plimsoll Mark, the permitted loading-line, and so, for ill-found and under-manned vessels, aggravated the risks of foundering in heavy weather. It was in 1876 that Samuel Plimsoll, 'the sailors' friend', persuaded Parliament to pass the Merchant Shipping Act which, among other statutory rules for safety, ordained a maximum load-line; and thirty years later, in a new Shipping Act, Lloyd George deepened the line and reduced the freeboard of too many unpainted tramps that lurched out of the Bristol Channel into the sudden storms of the Bay of Biscay. By seafaring men — and even more so, I fancy, by their wives — it was widely assumed that Lloyd George had been bribed by an unprincipled minority of Cardiff shipowners to introduce the Bill, and he and they were hotly denounced for their greed and irresponsibility.

I grew up in a house where there was little sympathy with Liberal measures, and none at all for Liberal leaders. It was, moreover, a temporary habitation. As soon as possible — as soon as my father should be transferred to a trade- route whose home ports were elsewhere than the Bristol Channel — we should go back to Scotland.

from *Fanfare for a Tin Hat* (1970)

JACK JONES

A Royal Visit

When at last Edward came into his Kingdom and Empire he remembered
Cardiff and after a while he graciously raised its status to that of a city.
Then our old friend Dan Regan departed in peace, and his funeral was
most impressive. Beside him in the coffin was the navvy's shovel with the
blade sharpened and thin with all the work he had done with it on the
making of Cardiff's first dock. Proud he was of his old shovel, and he made
Gwenny promise that it should be buried with him. "That's all I want to
take with me. I'll go with my left hand in Letty's and my shovel in my
right hand to meet my God. Her old Paddy and merciful God's old
navvy . . .".

The breath left him and Gwenny closed his eyes and that, dear reader,
was that. Cardiff a city, and the old navvy who greatly helped in the
making of it had left the world with only the shovel with which he had
come to Cardiff so many years ago. Nearly seventy years ago, sixty-seven,
to be precise. The shovel he brought to Cardiff was all he took out of it
when he died, leaving the money he had made and everything else that
had been his to others.

And now . . . yes, now, in 1907, and the era of our gallant and gay if
rather short-winded King Edward VII in full bloom. When we think of
all that has happened in Cardiff alone since he ascended the Throne it
seems incredible. When he arrives to-morrow, with the Queen and
Princess Victoria, he will find it hard to believe his own eyes. For the new
City of Cardiff has a new look and a new atmosphere and is prouder of
itself than the old town of Cardiff was. Electric trams run along the main
roads, on which there are now almost as many motor cars as horse-drawn
vehicles.

Ever so much more might be said of the progress, peace and prosperity
of the twentieth-century Edwardian era — long may it last, say the vast
majority of the people of Cardiff. "God save him," say the Irish who claim
to be in the majority of a population now surely nearing the two hundred
thousand mark. That alone is most amazing, for when the late Dan Regan
first came to Cardiff in 1838, not quite seventy years ago, the population
of the little town with only a canal and stage-coaches running into and out
of it was only ten thousand. To-morrow, with the people brought into it

41

by the three railway companies serving the city, there will be anything up to three hundred thousand people in the city to welcome their Majesties and the Princess Victoria. Between the upper and lower decks of each and every tram-car on the roads, right along the whole length, run big letters asking God to save our King.

All streets and buildings are decorated in readiness for to-morrow, and amongst the many new buildings are several which will almost certainly impress their Majesties and H.R.H. Princess Victoria. The City Hall itself, set like a jewel in Cathays Park, the site which the late and the present Marquesses of Bute, on the advice of the all-powerful Sir William Thomas Lewis, conditionally allowed Cardiff to have and hold for its new Civic Centre.

An avenue lined with infant trees, the avenue which the King will open, God willing, to-morrow, is all that separates the new Law Courts from the new City Hall, both buildings similar in design. On the south-eastern corner of the park, which is such an admirable site for the new Civic Centre, is Robert Redford's magnificent New Theatre, and — if we attempt to list even without describing all Cardiff's new buildings and developments we shall not finish doing so in time to welcome their Majesties to-morrow.

The Right Hon. D. Lloyd George, M.P., President of the Board of Trade in the Liberal Ministry which is now settling down to its task of cleaning up after the Tories, recently described the new City Hall and Law Courts — taken in their setting and surroundings — as "the finest municipal pile of buildings in the kingdom". Whether "pile" is the right word in this connection is perhaps doubtful, but the only Welshman in the Liberal Cabinet was reported to have used the word in an interview with a reporter who had accosted him after the annual banquet of the Cardiff Chamber of Commerce, this being the first occasion on which such a banquet had been held in the magnificent Assembly Room of the City Hall.

Mr Lloyd George was the guest of honour at this banquet and as such he spoke very well indeed on 'Trade and Commerce'. Two M.P.'s, the Hon. Ivor Guest, now Member for Cardiff, and Mr Clifford Cory, a Cardiff man who represented a Cornish division in the House of Commons, followed the Rt. Hon. gent. and proposed toasts. In proposing the toast of the City of Cardiff, Mr Cory proudly referred to himself as a son of Cardiff and went on to say that in the world of trade and commerce "Cardiff coal had beaten all others . . .".

After such a wonderful banquet some allowance must be made for exaggeration. There was no such thing as "Cardiff coal", not a fraction of an ounce of it had ever existed. The coal he referred to as "Cardiff coal" was "shipped" from Cardiff but it was hard got out of the coalfield which was deep down under the feet of the hills miles distant from Cardiff.

The Hon. Ivor Guest, M.P., proposed the toast of the Cardiff Chamber of Commerce. He said they were gathered together at a time of great prosperity for Cardiff's staple trade, the coal trade. As Liberal Member for Cardiff he was proud to think. . . .

He went on to speak of the coal trade as Cardiff's and without reference to the hewers of it, the South Wales miners who were now demanding a wage increase which was being considered by the South Wales Colliery Owners, who at this time could afford to be generous. For there was at this time what Cardiff's newspapers delighted in calling A GREAT BOOM IN COAL. The market was still excited and prices were still advancing when the news of the death of John Boyle, at the advanced age of eighty-eight, reached Cardiff from where the old man lived in Somerset.

Cardiff, speaking generally, had almost forgotten the man who for nearly thirty years had spoken and acted for and on behalf of the third Marquess of Bute. But Sir William Thomas Lewis, Boyle's successor as Agent-in-Chief and spokesman for the Bute Estate, had never forgotten the man under whom he had gained the experience necessary for the administration of a great and ever-growing estate.

The news of old Boyle's passing made Sir William feel both old and sad at a time when things were going better than at any time before. He was soon to have the honour, with the young Marquess — who, by the way, has made an excellent marriage — of receiving their Majesties the King and Queen, and also Princess Victoria. It was to open another Bute enterprise, the Queen Alexandra Dock, that their Majesties were coming to Cardiff — the opening of the King Edward the Seventh Avenue in Cathays Park was a secondary affair. The main purpose of the royal visit would be the opening of the great dock — and to commemorate that and that alone Sir William, with the full approval of the Marquess, had decided that a special medal should be struck. "We may allow the City Council the credit for it after we've made certain that it will be done, my lord . . .".

But Sir William is seventy and his beard and moustache are white and after hearing of the decease of his predecessor in office he felt depressed. But not for long. Pride soon conquered depression. Fifty-eight years of hard work from the age of twelve had brought him to where he was, had made him the power he now was in this infant city. He felt he had every right to feel proud. Modern Cardiff, he felt, was partly his creation. What was there to justify his pride?

All around the Castle and ancient Keep, and the walls with ancient Roman footing was the modern twentieth-century city with its mushroom manifestations. Its three theatres, two music halls, concert- and dance-halls and halls in which animated pictures were now being shown nightly. There was a racecourse and the Rugby football ground, a ground now capable of accommodating forty thousand spectators. It was packed to capacity when international matches were played there. Miles of docks and from Cardiff one could go by rail or sea to any and every part of the world. Fast express trains had made London Cardiff's next-stop neighbour, and Cardiff businessmen could now return the same day after doing what business they had to do in London. Then London's business houses and leading businessmen and financiers had by now practically adopted the fast-growing and prospering and attractive City of Cardiff.

from *River out of Eden* (1951)

R.M. LOCKLEY

Blackberrying

In the August holidays there was the great event of blackberrying, when Mother led her brood far into the wilderness, to the mountain slopes and lonelier ravines less visited by suburban competitors. Her ambition: to fill the store room with inexpensively-made jam, enough to last the whole winter for the rising tide of pupils who paid for meals.

She would wake us early, make us put on old clothes while Bessie prepared our frugal breakfast of tea, porridge, bread and margarine, before she took the day off on her own. Baskets and buckets were packed with bottles of milk (sterilized by boiling) and weak lemonade, a dozen of the largest potatoes, loaves of bread, margarine, Welsh cakes, honey, sugar and tea. Mother packed her first-aid kit, including a tourniquet in case of adder-bite (there were plenty of two kinds of snake on the Wenallt's ferny, brambly slopes at this time of year).

Mother wore a large sun-bonnet, anxious to preserve her pale complexion — a sunburned face would be too vulgar and undignified in the headmistress of a private school of good repute. She carried a walking stick with a curved handle to hook within reach the ripe hazel nuts. In some places there would be whinberries: Babs was closest to the ground, her sharp eyes could pluck these low-growing, tiresome, but very sweet little fruits; and might we find a few late wild strawberries?

"What about crab-apples? I love crab-apple jelly," Aline asked.

"Hardly ripe, and such a weight to carry. We'll see how we get on. We need as many blackberries as we can pick."

To reach her favourite spot, far from more sluggish competitors, involved a march of four or five miles. Happy hours followed in which the older children competed to pick the heaviest weight of blackberries. Ronald ate too many, or chased after bird and butterfly, watchful for basking snakes, observing how the family of bullfinches fed daintily on the seeds of the scarlet campion, but with his basket half-empty in the crook of his arm.

Back we come at the thrice-repeated whistle by midday for the picnic under the trembling leaves of the silver birches by the babbling brook, its clear water used to fill the black gallon kettle (laboriously lugged all the way by Ken). Dead dry twigs first, laid across two lumpy stones, little red-

45

golden flames, then thicker sticks and branches snapped short, more smoke as the green ash (which burns well) is laid on. Suddenly the old kettle is boiling and blacker than ever.

A dipper or water-ouzel flits by, protesting at our presence in its territory, bobbing from a wet mossy boulder. Tea goes down well with the older members of our party, but. . . .

"All the lemonade's gone, Babs!" Drunk by long nips during the morning session. "Here's a clean handkerchief. Strain some water into the cup from the stream." Much more satisfying to lie flat in the sedges, break the reflection of your heated face in the mirror of a pool, and suck up the icy mountain water through parched lips.

The bread and margarine (first slice without honey) is ambrosia, seized and devoured, whole round after whole round, as fast as Mother, hot and momentarily care-free, can slice the big cottage loaf, pressed against that comforting bosom, with the worn carving knife. Ah, to stretch out in the green mountain grass and bracken afterwards, secure and replete with so much food and intimate company! Only the flies to bother you — drive them off with a wand of bracken.

Mother, her wispy greying hair teased by the breeze as her bonnet is cast aside in the shade of the birches; Mother, were you quite happy? Or did you at that moment remember your handsome gentlemanly Harry, he who should have husbanded, loved and cherished thee?

"Pity Father isn't here . . .".

"I've got a thorn, Mother."

"There's a grey wagtail flown up the stream. May have a late nest. Coming to look, Aline?"

There were moments when I was closer to Aline than the others, as I was in age; she was just twenty-one months my senior. Together in the holidays we had begun to invent a secret language — Little Welsh we called it, although it had no relation to that ancient Celtic tongue, but was laboriously devised on a random choice of syllables. Aline had begun to compile a dictionary, using the pages of an abandoned address book.

We wandered in search of the grey wagtail, then remembered to look for the spot where we had last year built a rough cabin of boughs in a nearby copse. It was nice to be alone with any one of my sisters, but especially Aline just now; Little Welsh had drawn us together, and Aline enjoyed monopolizing Ronald. There was a natural rivalry and jealousy between the sisters, a mild malicious satisfaction when one triumphed over the others in some small family intimacy. Aline liked to be different, a quiet enigmatic girl in the presence of her older sisters, resisting their sometimes nagging requests. She did everything or nothing well, no half-measures, she could be violently energetic and successfully athletic, or else as stationary as a limpet. Nothing would move her in this negative mood; her apparent obstinacy and introspection maddened the others. They considered in fact that Aline was Mother's favourite — which was of course unfair — but we grew to accept this situation.

Not until I was a grown man was I told that Aline had been a seven-months baby — that was said to be the reason — or excuse — for Mother's underlying anxiety to avoid upsetting her third-born daughter.

"Look out for snakes!" called Mother as we strolled away. "I'm going to have forty winks here in the shade. Everyone take an empty basket and be back here at the whistle for tea. Go with Enid, Babs . . .".

"Tea, with roast spuds!" I shouted, in gleeful anticipation.

"Ronald, how many times have I told you not to use that vulgar word! I suppose you copy it from your friend George Witcombe?"

The potatoes, buried under the hot ash and charcoal of the midday fire, were done to a mealy richness in their skins a few hours later. Delicious!

Total harvest of blackberries for the day: 43 lbs, weighed over the cookery scales by Bessie, who wrote down the approximate score in her galloping schoolgirl script: Mrs L, Enid and Kate each 8, Ken 6, Aline 5, Ron and Babs each 4.

I was ashamed, but Mother was triumphant. She had also gathered a basket full of hazel nuts.

"A splendid day's work!" she declared.

That evening there was the inevitable sickly-sweet smell of boiling, bubbling berries, which hung around the house for days. We envisaged once more endless rows of jam jars on the store-room shelves, refilled with the knobbly berries, here and there an overlooked stewed grub and indigestible thorny sprig. I have never cared for blackberry jam since.

from *Myself When Young* (1979)

JOHN STUART WILLIAMS

Gwynt Traed y Meirw

The dead-foot wind creeps from the east
its razor open wide.
It shaves the people from the streets
and wipes them off inside.

The signboard of the Butcher's Arms
clicks sadly in the air.
The bar shines like a coffin-lid,
you'll find no comfort there.

An empty bus runs like a hearse
upon the blackened road.
Though no one sits upon its seats
it carries an icy load.

So put your sheepskin jacket on,
your cosy fur lined boots;
muffle up your winter fears,
the sap's shrunk to the roots.

However warm your secret thoughts,
whatever you've been told
by fat psychiatrist or priest,
the feet of the dead are cold.

W.C. ELVET THOMAS

A People Apart

When my mother came to Alexandra Road, Cardiff, to live, and I just a nine months old baby, she found that my father had furnished the whole house ready for her to take possession of it, and though it looks rather ordinary today it was a good house according to the standards of those days. There were four rooms on the ground floor and a huge pantry, and upstairs there were three good bedrooms and an excellent bathroom. The greatest blessing for any mother was the taps, cold water and hot water taps upstairs and in the kitchenette, and for one who had had to fetch water from the well a hundred yards from the house when at home in Ffynnonstown these taps were a great boon. There were some other advantages. There was no need to go far to go shopping, indeed there were three little shops nearby, one on the corner of 'our' street. One of these little shops was kept by an old English woman by the name of Mrs Ashcroft, and when she came to know that my father took part in *eisteddfodau* — that was something honourable in her sight, though her knowledge of such things, certainly, was very vague — she had to tell her nephew, who visited her occasionally, about us and brought him along to see us. That nephew was Dr (later Sir) Henry Coward, the famous musician and critic who was greatly interested in the Welsh people. Probably my father enlightened him about several of his ideas about Wales.

The change from the countryside of Pembrokeshire to Cardiff was a tremendous one for my mother. Here she was now in the midst of a sea of English, an alien in her own country, and everything strange and new to her as far as *living* was concerned. It is true that she had stayed in my father's lodgings for some months before, but here she was now compelled 'to settle down' and organise things as best she could herself. Her longing for her old home was overwhelming at times but she was very fortunate in her neighbours. A family by the name of Preston lived on one side of us, and a widow with a son and daughter by the name of Pitman on the other side — all English, but they were especially kind to my mother, the young Welsh woman who was not yet accustomed to life in a city. The Preston family were of immense help to her. Mr Preston's great interest was gardening, and as my mother was a bit of a specialist on the subject it helped to develop a friendship between him and his family and us. We were sorry when they left and took a house at the top of Leckwith hill, out in the country. There was enough scope there for Mr Preston to practise his hobby. They were neighbours of ours for some years.

After them came a young Jewish couple, the husband from Poland (and one look at him was enough to proclaim his race), and his beautiful wife from Bessarabia in Southern Russia. The wife's English was very broken and because my mother found it easy to make friends, *she* could now help the young Jewess. They were orthodox Jews and their appreciation of every good turn was great. Every Friday night, when it became dark, we could see them lighting the candles — their custom to show that their Sabbath had begun. They went regularly to the synagogue and celebrated every one of the festivals of their religion. Feasting was often part of the celebration, and because they were of a generous nature no feast occurred without plenty of fruit and delicacies passing over the garden wall for us. When the Feast of the Unleavened Bread came we, too, had plenty of the bread from them. It is often said that the Jews are miserly but we found them otherwise. One day, when our neighbour was talking to my mother, my mother noticed that she had a lovely ruby ring on one of her fingers, and when my mother expressed her admiration of it the Jewess took it from her own finger and put it on my mother's. "Keep it", she said, "as a small token of my appreciation of your kindness". That ring was on my mother's finger for years. I have an idea that the Jews next door felt that there was something different about us. They were newcomers from the continent. They knew nothing about Wales but realised that we were not English, and because of that they felt, I believe, a kind of "affinity" with us. We too, though we were in our own country, were a people apart, aliens in the community — if community indeed — in which we now lived. A daughter was born to our neighbours but she died when she was about three years old. She died about eight o'clock at night and was in her grave by noon next day. My mother was invited to the funeral service next door. She understood nothing of what the Rabbi said, but what surprised her most was seeing women sitting on cushions on the floor and wailing loudly and beating their breasts. Better days came to this family of Jews. A son was born to them and great was the rejoicing and celebrating, and we again had a share of the delicacies especially on the important day when the little son was circumcised. To our grief these Jews were not neighbours of ours much longer. They moved to another part of the city but others came to take their place and they too were kind. . . .

One autumn morning, when I was about five years of age my mother took me to the Infants' School in Severn Road. After going through the business of being registered officially by the headmistress I was left there, a monoglot little Welshman, in the midst of a horde of English children. Strangely enough, I do not remember that I felt anything odd because I could not understand the language of the other children. I was left completely alone. What struck me most was the clothes of some of the children. It is literally true that some of them, especially the boys, wore rags and several were not too clean and their rags stank from afar. My greatest fear was that I would have to sit beside one of these stinking ragged ones. Very luckily I was put to sit beside a boy who was clean enough, although he looked rather poor. It is obvious to me, as I look back, that many of the children suffered because of the poverty and environment of their homes. They knew nothing about the innumerable advantages of today's children.

I must have come to understand English almost at once. It is quite likely that I had, unconsciously, assimilated a lot of English into my constitution. Although it was Welsh only that was spoken in the house at home, yet, outside the door, it was English only I heard and so it is certain that I had already been conditioned to take English for granted, However, from the very start, I had no difficulty in following the lessons and enjoying them. Every lesson was of course in English, and in this school I never heard Wales mentioned nor the Welsh language. But one day I was made to begin to think that there was something special in the fact that I spoke Welsh. I was taken by one of the teachers to see the headmistress of the Girls' School. She could speak a little Welsh. I was introduced to her and then, after we exchanged a few words in Welsh, I was taken back to the Infants' School. Her Majesty, the Headmistress of the Girls' School, had now met the specimen of a Welshman who had appeared in the Infants' School.

The day I remember most is the day Empire Day was celebrated, May 24, the scarcely mentionable *Empire Day*. This was a day close to the heart of Miss Dawson, the headmistress. The school hall was adorned with innumerable flags — small Union Jacks by the hundred, to my mind, and the flags of all the countries of "the empire on which the sun never set" — every flag, it seemed to me, except the flag of Wales, there was not as much as one Red Dragon. The climax of the celebration was an address by the headmistress on the privilege of belonging to such a splendid empire and

51

our duty always to be loyal to it. There was a lot of singing 'patriotic' songs, like 'Rule Britannia', and the children enjoyed themselves bellowing another song —

Flag of Britain proudly waving
Over many distant seas.

Then, turning towards a large Union Jack beside Miss Dawson, we had to make a kind of salute and shout at the top of our voices

We *salute* thee
And we pray
God to bless our land today.

The children too had some unofficial rhymes but only one of these — the children's favourite, obviously — has remained in my memory. Although Victoria had been in her grave for years the children continued to say:

It's the twenty-fourth of May,
The Queen's birthday;
If we don't get a holiday
We'll all run away.

What, I wonder, would have been the effect on me had I stayed longer in Miss Dawson's school and heard more of the imperial babble? However that may be, the medical examination day arrived and it was discovered that I had an ailment which could only be cured by surgery or a long stay in the fresh air of the country. My mother believed that one should 'avoid the knife' if possible, and therefore there was nothing for it but to write to her parents, and without any ado I went to stay for a period in the paradise of Ffynnonstown.

By the time I returned to Cardiff a new school had been opened, namely Kitchener Road School, and since this school was nearer our house than Severn Road School, it was decided that I was to go to the new school. This was a much better school, its cleanliness and newness was a wonder, in comparison with the old buildings of Severn Road. As far as I was concerned there was one other great difference. By now my brother Arthur was old enough to start school and both of us were taken to the Babies' Department — the 'Infants' again. By now I was an old hand at English and found no difficulty in holding my own: but as for Arthur, he knew only next to nothing. He could not understand his teacher and she could not understand him. More than that, four year old Arthur hated to hear English, and when the teacher asked him to say an English word he insisted on making it sound Welsh. If there was any success made in conveying the meaning of an English word to him he would not use that word but would anglicise the Welsh form of the word, for example, he refused to use the English word *oven* although he knew it. If he had to refer to oven, and he saw no reason for doing so, well, the teacher had to be satisfied with the anglicised form of the Welsh *ffwrn*, namely *furn*. The word *furn* was good enough for Arthur and if the teacher did not accept that word why should he worry? Between Arthur's obstinacy and the teacher's ignorance in matters linguistic things went from bad to worse. But there was refuge and that was Miss Roberts the headteacher. She could speak Welsh, and it was with her in her room that Arthur spent part of his time at first. She alone could understand him. Miss Roberts must have had a special talent, for it was through her that Arthur was able "to settle down" and make the best of the alien education given to him. The youngest children were taught through play, and because there were all kinds of toys which were clean and new, Arthur enjoyed himself, and because he was naturally cheerful and happy (as he was throughout his life), he became a favourite with everybody. Yet, in that school, out of hundreds of children there was no one except the two of us who were Welsh-speaking. In spite of that we were quite happy. In my class the main work was learning to read English. To my amazement I realised that I could read simple English as easily as whistle, and that many of my English fellow pupils found the work exceedingly difficult. I do not remember learning to read. Somehow or other I became conscious that I could read Welsh and English. Maybe my mother had taught me very early but I have no recollection of her doing so.

There was no Welsh nor any mention of Wales in this school again. I have no recollection that we sang as much as a single Welsh song and I do not believe that we celebrated St David's Day as such. Yet I do remember one day in the drawing lesson when we were asked to draw a picture of something *Welsh* — a leek or a daffodil or the 'Welsh' hat or the Prince of Wales' feathers. It was not on paper that we drew our pictures but either on the wall with coloured chalks or on the glass of the windows with bits of dry soap. There was enough glass for us to practise our soap talent, and the lower part of the walls of the room were made of long dark slates placed so that the younger children could reach them and use them. It is possible that we were celebrating St David's Day by drawing those pictures. It is likely that there was some kind of celebrating in the 'Big Boys' school. One morning I was taken by one of the teachers to the 'Big Boys' school, and in we went to the hall where the whole school had gathered. I was led to a little platform where the headmaster, Mr Trewartha, was standing. Without a moment's warning I was asked could I recite something Welsh. Luckily I did have a recitation (I am not sure, but it is quite possible that it was 'Nant y Mynydd'), and I recited the poem. Judging by their hand-clapping I must have given pleasure to my listeners. The headmaster was pleased too and gave me a penny for my trouble. I had not yet begun to take part in *eisteddfodau*, and this penny was the first money I ever had for doing something publicly in Welsh. And the value of a penny in those days was not something to be sniffed at either. In those days it was much more substantial than it is today. One could buy a whole pound of sweets for fourpence and I knew very well a little shop near the school where I could get, for my penny, a quarter of a pound of the most glorious mints.

The days of the Infants' School — a mixed school — came to an end, and one morning I and a crowd of other boys of the same age were transferred to the 'Big Boys' school. A new headmaster had come to this school, short, paunched, thickset and the most arrant of Englishmen. He had one great virtue, he kept to his room and we seldom saw him. He sent for me one day to tell me that my work was very satisfactory, and if I continued to do work that pleased him *maybe* I should see a photograph of myself on the wall, since his intention was to have a gallery of tiny photographs of the boys who 'did well' in school work. As it happened I had no chance at all to see whether I was worthy of the honour of the gallery. All the plans of the headmaster were ruined by changes which came in the wake of the First World War. One of the results of the war was to convert Kitchener Road School into a hospital and it was arranged that the children of Kitchener Road and their teachers were to be sent to Severn Road School. The buildings of Severn Road, of course, could not contain the children and teachers of two schools and it was decided by the authorities that the following plan had to be adopted — the two schools to share the buildings. It was arranged that one school was to use them in the morning and the other in the afternoon — the one which came in the morning one week to come in the afternoon the following week and so on every alternate week. This meant, of course, that we had either the morning or the afternoon free every day and I, at least, had no cause for complaint about that. There was I, now, though. I was one of the Kitchener Road pupils, back again where I began, in the Severn Road School old buildings. My school days at this time were very happy days. Every day was a real joy, and that probably because I was lucky enough to have a particularly gifted teacher in J.E.P. Naylor. Although he had, I believe, a degree of the University of Wales, I never heard him referring to Wales nor anything Welsh and he knew no Welsh. In spite of that he knew how to give lessons in English and he understood boys. He was one of the very few teachers to whom I am sure I am indebted, and it gives me pleasure to have this opportunity of acknowledging as much. . . .

Although the majority of the children knew that Arthur and I could speak Welsh and that we spoke Welsh with one another, that made no difference to their attitude towards us, and on the whole we had a happy enough childhood in our dealings with other children. My parents were most anxious about the effect associating with other children would have upon us and especially upon our Welsh, and there is no denying that they had good cause for anxiety. Seldom did Arthur and I speak English to each other even in the company of other children but we did so sometimes. My mother one day happened to come by and heard us speaking English to each other. She came to us and packed us home unceremoniously. After we reached the house we were sharply rebuked. Never were there offenders before the bench who trembled more than the two of us did on that day when mother made us understand, without mincing words, that henceforth we were to speak Welsh to each other at all times. I am glad to say that we never afterwards transgressed. One had to be firm to keep the Welsh language. It would have been easy enough to allow the language, through neglect, to vanish from our lips. And that is what happened, more's the pity, in many a family in Cardiff. Backbone and constant watchfulness were necessary on the part of parents in those days — and the same is necessary today — to keep the language. Fortunately for us, their children, our parents realised that the Welsh language was one of the most valuable treasures they could give to us, and they were determined that we were not to lose our heritage through any neglect on their part.

My parents knew very well that there was a considerable difference between us and many of the children with whom we played. For one thing, our home was full of books and we took Welsh and English papers and periodicals regularly. The homes of many of the other children were homes without books. The red *Cymru, Cymru'r Plant* and *Tywysydd y Plant* came to our house every month. My father read *Y Beirniad* and *Y Genhinen*

55

too. We received English papers like Arthur Mee's *Children's Newspaper*, and were allowed to read the *Magnet* and *Gem* and the popular comics. Lest we laid too much stress on the English things it was my father's custom to question us about the contents of *Cymru'r Plant* and we had to prove to his satisfaction that we had read it.

We were faithful to the chapel *and* to Sunday School and in that way also we were different from many of the other children. Many of them too used to go to Sunday Schools when Whit Monday or Christmas were approaching, but few of them thought of attending a service in chapel or church.

Although our neighbours' children were ready to accept us into their midst all the adults were not as favourably inclined. One day, when I was about eight years old and Arthur six, we were playing in the street and of course we were speaking Welsh to each other. Some strange woman came up to us and asked me, "Were you two talking Welsh?" "Yes", said I. "Well, take that!" said she, giving me a hard slap across my cheek which made me totter. Then she walked haughtily away thinking, I'm sure, that she had taught a lesson to a little Welsh devil. And indeed she *had* taught me a grim lesson. From that day I knew that the Welsh language had its enemies not only in the schools but also in the big world outside the schools. Although I was so young I was beginning to understand my parents' firm stand on behalf of the Welsh language and I felt very proud of them also. I was coming to realise gradually that their Welshness was a rock which would not move whatever storms beat upon it. I mentioned previously the journalist Howard Spring, who became famous as an English novelist. He was born in Canton, Cardiff, in a poor home in a very poor back street not far from Salem Welsh Chapel. Though he was brought up in Cardiff and though he is so talented and so sensitive to his environment, neither Wales nor the Welsh language meant anything to him. That was not his fault but that of the community in which he was brought up. Had it not been for my parents' care I too, quite probably, would be fully as ignorant of Wales and of the Welsh language as he.

translated by the author. from *Tyfu'n Gymro* (1972)

ALUN LLYWELYN-WILLIAMS

When I was Young

All day and every day the sea shone, steeped in its blueness;
the sun foresaw no storms of tomorrow, wept no yesterday's guilt:
I walked the quay in the white morning, questioning masts,
prying and spying under the swoop of raucous gulls
till there was my *Gwennan Gorn*, my spray whelp, my sea-spearer.

I would lie in the boat's prow and trail my hands in the water;
nearing the unbearable purity of the island lighthouse,
where the fish swayed and sped under the soundless rock;
how gaily the sail leapt to the blue heavens,
how prettily then it sank to the depth of my daring sinews!

The green land hung like a dream between the eyelids,
the furrows of the sea never counted the youthful hours of my course:
harsh on returning, it was to tread the unheaving earth,
to traverse the heavy clay,
and to hear, now from its cell, the mortal knell of the flesh.

A return without returning: those suns wore
to their late long setting; but the darkling light over the bay
stays on, as though some miracle had snatched to that virginal tower
the warming eye of the world:
and, just as before time's watchmen besieged me, it shines
still on a voyage unfinished.

translated by Gwyn Williams

GORONWY REES

Growing Up

My family's move to Cardiff brought about an almost total trans-
formation in the way I had lived until then. To some extent this was true
for all my family, but less so, I think, than in my own case, because they
were older and had some experience of the world outside Aberystwyth,
which for me was still the only world there was. My elder sister was ten
years older than I. She had already taken a degree at Aberystwyth, and
shortly after we moved took up a teaching post in Barry. My younger
sister was looking forward to getting married shortly, and her eyes were
exclusively directed towards Briton Ferry, where her future husband, also
an ex-student of Aberystwyth, was attempting to learn his way in the steel
industry.

As for my brother, Cardiff was for him only a brief staging post, at
which to matriculate before returning to Aberystwyth, where the
university at that time possessed an excellent law school; for he was to be a
barrister, as my father had once intended to be, and was already single-
mindedly determined to begin his legal studies as quickly as possible. He
was a clever boy, and it was normal at that time for Aberystwyth's best
law students to proceed to Cambridge after taking their degree.

But for me Cardiff was to be the place in which I spent the whole of my
adolescence, as different from childhood as Cardiff itself was from
Aberystwyth, and perhaps I associate it with unhappiness both because of
the confusion and turbulence of such a phase in one's life and because our
migration seemed to bring an end to the warmth and security of the close
knit family life we had hitherto enjoyed. It seemed to me that my brother
and sisters had grown up and had already entered, or stood at the
threshold of, the world of men and women of which I knew nothing, while
I was left behind in some grey and mournful limbo of my own, from which
all the familiar landmarks of the past had been obliterated. And I think
that, in a curious way, my parents had something of the same feeling, with
their children growing up and away from them and their own lives so
greatly changed from what they had known before.

For my mother especially, who was essentially a country girl, the city of
Cardiff always remained as faceless, anonymous and characterless as it
was to me; and to her, as to me, the change from the rural atmosphere of

Aberystwyth, which was hardly more than a large seaside village, to the great city which Cardiff was by comparison, was a change from community to loneliness. Indeed, the change made itself felt even in our house, for in my later years in Cardiff, when I lived alone with my father and mother for most of the year, it seemed as if the house were empty and deserted, as if we inhabited some melancholy solitude together. . . .

I was too young, or too selfish, to understand the changes involved for my parents by moving to Cardiff; or perhaps I was at first too much taken up in my own sense of deprivation, and when that passed too preoccupied by new interests, to notice what was happening to others. For to me at first the loss of my childhood world, so tiny and circumscribed, yet somehow open to all the seas and skies of the world, was a shock that was almost traumatic. I felt as if I had been cast out of paradise, and with a sense not of loss only, but of guilt, as if somehow it was my own fault. Most of all I missed a certain quality of perception which, in my childhood, had seemed to make everything at once familiar and magical and now, under the shock of removal to the city, seemed to wither away like some fabulous plant that would only blossom in its native soil.

For my first, yet enduring impression was of the unrelieved ugliness of the city, of its long grey streets and the monotonously repeated vistas of identical terrace houses, the muddy complexion of its stones and the hideously flaring red and orange of its bricks that inflicted themselves on one's sight like a wound. They affected one's eyes like some painful ailment, as if they had been rubbed sore by seeing. To me this world which man had built for himself seemed utterly inhuman, hostile to all the innumerable responses of the nerves and the senses, while the natural world which pressed so closely upon one in Aberystwyth had been so perfectly attuned to every infinitesimal impulse that it seemed to fit one like a glove.

I had never been to a city of any size before and its wastes of brick and mortar weighed upon me with a dull sense of oppression that was like a physical pain. It was years before I realized that even city landscapes can have their own beauty and certainly there was little of this to be seen in Cardiff. Walking or cycling to school through the long grey tunnel of Mackintosh Place in which every grey little house faithfully reproduced the hideousness of its neighbour, or down the tramlines of the City Road where neither the shops nor the objects offered for sale in them had any quality or virtue except the grimmest utility, I would feel a sense of leaden hopelessness, as if these streets stretched on into infinity and there would never be any escape from them, mathematically parallel lines projecting the city and its inhabitants in an endless future of which every moment was nothing but the exact and senseless repetition of what came before and after it. Sometimes I could hardly believe that the sea, blue, smiling, and welcoming, was not awaiting round the corner and it was with a sense of doom, as of a condemned man, that I realized there lay before me only another monotonous perspective of the no-man's-land of the city.

In those first years in Cardiff I began to feel, for the first time, that destructive sense of depression which reduced the whole of life to a uniform monochrome and transforms every impulse to thought or action into the meaningless reflex of a mechanical puppet. It is a sense which has frequently recurred to me in later years; for those who feel it, it is so acute that it eats like acid into the texture of life, so that it falls away from one in shreds and tatters, like some threadbare garment which has worn so thin that it can no longer hold together. And whether or not it was the fact of our removal that induced my depression at that time, or whether it had its roots in deeper causes, it is true that for a year or two I underwent some mysterious form of sea-change, some hidden revolution in the depths of the self, which coloured all my experiences and made them so dark, confused, and fragmentary that they hardly seemed to be mine at all.

We cannot truly see what is happening in the darkest recesses of the self, nor can memory accurately reproduce what is so fitfully and partially perceived. Perhaps it would be better simply to say that for a time I felt totally disorientated in the new world we had entered, stumbling about in it awkwardly and childishly as if my limbs were no longer under my own control and my feet no longer knew where they were carrying me.

For at first it was a world of strangers, and the boys I met in my new school seemed to me so different from those I had known before that they hardly seemed to belong to the same race. And indeed to a large extent they did not, because Cardiff is as much an English as a Welsh city, a mongrel border town in which the Welsh strain has been so diluted as to produce a far more variegated social pattern than I was accustomed to. But to me at least the boys in my school were alike in that they were all different from me, and in particular in being, or appearing, infinitely more mature and sophisticated, with the sharper wits and quicker intelligence of the town dweller, and the adaptability that came of living in a more complicated social structure than Cardiganshire had to offer. They laughed at my country accent, and even more at the curious garments my mother had constructed for me from a cast-off suit of one of my uncles, with trousers that hung well below the knee to allow for growth and a high buttoned jacket that might have been fashionable today but then had more than a touch of the grotesque. I had been proud of the suit when I first wore it, because the material was excellent and it had been tailored by mother's own hands, but now I quickly and shamefully realized that in the town it made me an object of ridicule and mockery. So perhaps it was not surprising that for some time I found it difficult to adapt myself to my new school. My brother, who had a better character and a more single-minded purpose than I, appeared to escape such difficulties and continued to achieve the same excellent academic results as ever; I on the other hand failed lamentably. In Aberystwyth I had been thought a bright boy, as became the son of my father; but in Cardiff I tended towards the bottom of my form with such consistency that my mother's ambitions for me seemed to be more absurd than ever. Indeed, even she began to lose faith, and when, at the end of my second year in the High School, I returned home with a report which was more than usually unsatisfactory, and my brother with one which was, by contrast, of almost dazzling achievement, my mother burst out into tears and confessed that she could not see what was to become of me. "If you go on like this", she said amid her tears, "you'll never be anything better than a bank clerk."

A bank clerk! It was a curious threat, for in those days when any form of employment was hard to come by in South Wales, to be a bank clerk might seem to promise an enviable future to almost any boy, secure, relatively well paid by our modest standards, and with the assurance of an eminently respectable social status. Yet my mother was right, and to me her words were words of doom; for to me as to my mother they signified a life of dull-minded devotion to commerce and the worship of Mammon, unilluminated by any higher interest, and neither she nor I thought that was a life worth living. As for me, I had already formed a quite different conception of what my life was to be, though if my mother had known of it she might have been no less dismayed than by the future with which she had threatened me. For I had already decided that by some means or other I would become a writer, though how this was to be achieved I could not guess, nor had I any reason for thinking that I possessed any of the talents it would require. In my eyes, there could be nothing more incompatible with a writer's life than the to me infinitely dreary calculations of profit and loss which I supposed to be the exclusive occupation of a banker.

But however vague my ideas of how I was to satisfy my literary ambitions, or even, indeed, of what it really means to be a writer, they were already sufficiently clear to make me face the choice which presents itself to every young Welshman with the same heritage and upbringing as myself; it was the choice of whether to write in English or Welsh, either of which at that time, would still have been possible to me. Nor was this simply a choice between two languages, entailing no further consequences. For every language has its own particular genius, and the language which one writes and speaks also very largely dictates what one thinks and what one feels. There are things that can be said in Welsh that cannot be said in English, just as there are things which can be said in English that cannot be said in Welsh, and in choosing a language one is not only choosing a vocabulary and a syntax but what one can say with them. Otherwise, the problem of translation would not remain the almost insoluble one that it is.

Today I feel surprised that, given my attachment to the scenes and language of my childhood, I should have made the choice so easily, almost without thinking, as if, for me at least, no choice was really necessary. Indeed, I can distinctly remember the moment when I made it. When I was fifteen, my Welsh master in school, himself a minor poet in his own language, asked me what I wished to be when I grew up. I answered that I wished to be a writer. "In Welsh or in English?" he asked; and went on to explain that a writer in English, which is a universal language, must expect to meet the most intense competition, which only the most talented could hope to survive, while in Wales, which has no professional writers and all are amateurs, the field was narrowly confined, and given any talent at all I could hardly fail to make some name for myself.

The advice was well meant, and I have no doubt that my Welsh master may well have been in the right; certainly he had my best interests at heart. But it was an unfortunate argument to use to a boy, and it was all the less attractive in the mouth of a patriotic Welshman. I have no doubt that, in a sense, and without knowing it, I turned my back upon Wales at that moment and since then I have had no reason to regret it. For literature then was already becoming for me something that is more important than nationality, a means of release from a way of life that had begun to seem cramped and constrained, and the key to some wider world than Wales had to offer. It was as if, in choosing the language of my childhood, I should have chosen to remain a child for ever, and this is something Welshmen often do. As for me, I felt that in leaving Cardiganshire I had left the happiness of childhood behind and, even if I wished, could not have it again. The trouble was, I suppose, that I wanted to grow up and felt that I could not do it in Welsh.

It was not ambition that made me want to be a writer, nor any belief in my literary talents, for this I have always lacked. It was the thought that outside there lay a wider world in which there were larger issues at stake than those which obsessed us in the narrow circle in which I had been brought up, where everything seemed certain and predictable and one might live and die without encountering more than a very few of the infinite varieties of human experience. It wasn't that one wanted to compete with others; one wanted to compete with oneself and see what one was capable of, like a gambler who will never leave the table until he has lost everything.

It is difficult now to unravel the labyrinthine workings of a boy's mind, partly because at the time one was largely unaware of one's motives and even now they have hardly become more clear. But somehow I date to this period, somewhere between my fifteenth and sixteenth year, a kind of awakening out of the mood of depression, compounded of nostalgia and apathy, into which I was thrown by my parents' move to Cardiff.

It helped to save me, at a time when I myself doubted whether I was worth saving, that my mother proved to be right in her instinct that, educationally at least, our migration to Cardiff would prove to be for my good. The High School at Cardiff at the time when I attended it, between 1923 and 1928, was indeed an excellent one, so good indeed that for me it still represents the ideal of what a school should be, and I still sometimes wonder at my good fortune in attending it. In the classics, in mathematics, in history and in English we were taught by men of quite exceptional ability and qualifications; my history master later held a university chair and became a Welsh historian of the greatest distinction.

I have often wondered since why men of such high intellectual capacity should have been content to devote themselves to the ungrateful task of teaching a somewhat rough and unruly set of boys. Partly, I suppose, it was because at that time schoolmastering as a profession provided a security and, especially in Wales, a social status which, alas, it no longer does, and a salary envied by many at a time and place where unemployment was a constant threat. But it was also because those men felt a genuine compulsion to impart their knowledge and their own high intellectual standards to their pupils, and this gave to their teaching a kind of urgency and passion which made education both an inspiration and a pleasure.

63

Most of all they were marvellously responsive to any sign of talent or ability and were wonderfully generous in the pains they took to foster it. They talked to one as if one were as adult and intelligent as they were; they answered one's questions and discussed the answers as if everything they said was only a basis for further questions; they lent one books and encouraged one's own interests; somehow one felt that the distinction between master and pupil ceased to have any importance compared with what was shared between them.

In all this we were the beneficiaries; and all the more because the school combined with its high standard of teaching an admirable freedom in matters of discipline, and for me, who was apt to resent any form of restraint, this was particularly fortunate. The headmaster, who looked rather more like a Prussian officer of the old school than a teacher, was himself only a moderate scholar, though he had a passion for the classics; but he had something which is even more valuable than scholarship in a schoolmaster, which was a deep and sincere respect for the individuality of every boy in his care, whether clever or stupid, docile or rebellious. There was little attempt at what is known as "character forming" and, outside their work, boys were left to become very much what they wanted to be. For the headmaster and his staff had grasped the essential truth that the larger part of life lies outside the walls of a school, and especially a day school like ours, and consciously or unconsciously they drew the conclusion that they could best serve their pupils by concentrating on the one function they were in a position to discharge most effectively; that is to say, the task of inculcating the highest intellectual standards which their pupils were capable of absorbing and of providing them with the basis of knowledge which they would require if they were to achieve either success or pleasure in life.

And curiously enough, by doing so they achieved, though by indirection, a far greater moral influence than if they had consciously attempted to shape and form that most elusive and amorphous of all natural phenomena, the character of an adolescent boy. For the process of learning, at any stage above the most elementary, has a moral value of its own, in which respect for truth is the greatest ingredient, and even boys are capable of absorbing it when properly taught; it is a kind of uncovenanted grace which is added to the other advantages and pleasures of learning. And perhaps something of this civilizing influence did make itself felt in the school. We were on the whole a rough lot, mostly of the lower middle class, and most of us were passionately addicted to Rugby football, which is not the most civilizing of pastimes; but there was very little of the cruelty or brutality, physical or mental, to which boys sometimes subject each other, or are subjected to by their teachers. If this was so, it was largely because of the staff, who were themselves humane and civilized men and were too interested in their teaching to have time to waste on the kind of petty persecution which sometimes goes by the name of discipline. I do not know what kind of verdict would be passed on the school if it were judged by modern educational standards. I imagine it might be said that it was too insistent on formal academic instruction, that it took things like examinations very seriously and prided itself on its academic record; yet in fact the education it gave was surprisingly wide and varied, and opened a boy's eyes to much broader intellectual vistas than the ordinary curriculum normally provides. Even today I am still surprised that our history master should have thought it worthwhile to include in his course a class in Plato's *Republic*, which was in fact an excellent introduction to philosophy; or that our English master should take me to his home to show me his excellent library and especially his fine editions of Blake and Donne, and by doing so inspire a lifelong devotion to both poets. He had once been a minor poet himself but was now a bibliophile and he did not care for the turn which modern poetry was taking; but when I, having found *The Waste Land* on the shelves of the Cardiff Public Library, announced my admiration of T.S. Eliot, he asked me to his home to explain to himself and a friend what were then still the mysteries of that poem. I do not know that I, a schoolboy with even less knowledge of life than of literature, made much of a job of my exposition; but I do know that, in my youthful and incoherent enthusiasm, I was listened to with as much interest and respect as if I had been Mr Eliot himself, and that at the end of a long evening's discussion of what the poem meant and of what it portended in the development of English poetry, I had learned far more than either of my sympathetic listeners.

Under such circumstances, learning becomes a pleasure and certainly it was largely due to the kind of education I received at school that after a time I began to struggle out of the mood of bewilderment and incomprehension induced by our moving to Cardiff, and that the acute sense of having lost the world of my childhood gradually diminished and gave way to the hope that perhaps, somewhere, life might again have to offer the same infinite possibilities which surrounded me as a child. Most boys, I think, in the process of growing up, suffer the same sense of

65

transition from one world to another and it is only accident which decides with what particular places or experiences it is identified, and accident also which decides with what degree of pain or difficulty the transition is made, or indeed whether it is made at all. For there are some unfortunate ones for whom the attachments of childhood are never overcome, and some for whom the pain and confusion of its passing never wholly cease, so that they remain for ever irretrievably fixed in a past which has never been transcended.

As for me, I was lucky, so much so indeed that for many years, until experience taught me otherwise, I was accustomed to think of myself as a favoured child of fortune. I was lucky in finding people who gave me a hand across the bridge which, poised so precariously above an abyss of doubts, confusions and uncertainties, leads from childhood to manhood. It was not only they who made the difference; but they helped as it were to dispel the mist which fogged my sight, so that at moments one might at least catch a glimpse of what the future might be. Certainly, so far as education was concerned, their encouragement was so far effective that my academic performance after a time began to inspire a hope that my mother's ambitions for me were not, after all, quite so absurd as they had once seemed. From about my sixteenth year, it began to be taken for granted that I should sit for a scholarship to Oxford, and preferably, because of the pleasure the gardens had once given my mother, to New College. . . .

On Saturday nights in winter, after playing football for the school in the afternoon, I would walk through Cardiff's streets, crowded with miners come down from the valleys to watch the match at Cardiff Arms Park and their wives enjoying the city's sights, and through the market near St John's Church where under their garish lights the stalls displayed the hot meat pies and black puddings and laverbread which were then the delicacies of the poor. The lights, the crowds, the drunks lurching out of the pubs, the girls waiting to be picked up made of Cardiff something entirely different from its drab every day; it was like walking on to the stage of a theatre in which everything has suddenly become much larger and brighter than life. I was already bemused and dazzled when I entered the cool mock-Gothic spaces of the library, but what lay within was no less enthralling than the scenes outside, and for a moment, in the entrance hall, I paused, almost dizzily poised between the real world and that other one which lay embalmed within the covers of the thousands of books that filled the library's shelves. . . .

During my last year at school I worked extremely hard, especially in the long winter evenings when I sat bent over my books at the table in our parlour while my mother and father read in silence in their armchairs on either side of the fireplace. The crimson tablecloth on which my books were piled, the glowing light of the fire, fed by the best Welsh coal, the dark mahogany furniture, and the Victorian prints on the walls, the scratching of my pen on the paper, the absolute and unbroken silence, induced in me a feeling that time had come to a stop and that we three were preserved for ever in an immobility which change could never threaten. And I was happy that it should be so, for the quiet room with its shadows in the corner where the lamplight never penetrated was transformed into a kind of enchanted cave peopled by all the spirits called up from the past by my books, which I read as if they were works of necromancy that could endow me with magical powers. If I paused for a moment and looked up from my reading, the sense of being encapsuled in some timeless moment, of total and absolute insulation against everything that existed outside those four walls, was so intense that I seemed to float free of my body and to look down on the room as if it were one of those Dutch interiors in which every worn and familiar object, and the faces of those who sit among them, are illuminated by an internal light, a warmth, a glow, a splendour that came from some world which is beyond the world of change.

This was in winter. In summer I worked alone in my bedroom and on golden evenings before the sun had finally set would allow myself the pleasure of walking through the gardens of the public park nearby to hire a boat and row for an hour on the shallow waters of its artificial lake. The park would be crowded with the citizens of Cardiff taking the evening air, trades people and their wives, courting couples, children bouncing balls and trundling hoops on the concrete paths between the symmetrically ordered flower beds, and the presence of so many others in a world which for me had become intensely solitary, the contrast with the dreams that filled my mind, momentarily bewildered and confused me, and yet this world of flesh and blood was as mysterious and alluring as anything the imagination had to offer. One evening I had been reading the *Lyrical Ballads*, and it seemed to me that it did not need the genius of a Wordsworth to infuse the light of poetry into the sober and somewhat drab reality of our municipal park, for it was not a light which we imagined or contrived for ourselves, as by some trick of stage production, but was as much a part of these men and women, these trees and flowers, these stretches of freshly watered grass in the yellowing evening sunshine as it had been of Adam and Eve as they walked in the garden of Eden.

The lake stretched beyond the gardens, and in the cool and mysterious shadows of the trees on the two small islands at its further end I let the boat float among the ducks that dabbled in its waters. One section of the lake was enclosed to form a bathing pool, where on warm evenings I used to swim and watch the slender long-legged bodies of the girls who swooped like swallows from the diving board and flashed like fish through the waters. To me they seemed like creatures out of mythology, nymphs, naiads, ondines, watersprites, and when sometimes I summoned up my courage to make their acquaintance I was tongue-tied with shyness and embarrassment and could find no words to express the confused desire which consumed me. I envied the boldness and brash confidence of my schoolfellows who, when darkness began to fall, would accompany the girls up the hill to the woods above the lake and next day regale the form with boasts of their sexual achievements. Only rarely did I overcome my shyness sufficiently to emulate their example, and then, lying in the grass beside a girl whose dark hair still wet from bathing hung down her back like a mermaid's, made clumsy attempts at love-making which only her more experienced hands, limbs, body, guided to success. But the memory of those girlish bodies — limbs that entwined one like seaweed, the smell as of fresh milk that exuded from their skin — haunted my dreams and blurred my vision as I sat bent over my books and they also had to be included in my vision of the world, in which almost everything else had been derived from literature and not from life.

from *A Chapter of Accidents* (1972)

GLYN JONES

A School in a Slum

I began teaching in a school in a long since cleared slum area near the centre of the city of Cardiff. The school population was, as always, mixed. Some children came from unexceptionable homes, clean, orderly, responsible, concerned, prepared to make sacrifices. Others, a very large number, perhaps even a majority, were surely among the poorest and most wretched in the city, ill fed, ill cared for, dressed in dirty, handed-on clothes often not much better than rags. Several came to school bare-footed even in winter, and many more, I often felt, would have been better off with their feet unshod than wearing the broken, sopping boots and stockings they had on. The parents of many of the children, even the apparently neglected ones, were good people often, who sent their children to school badly nourished and poorly dressed through no fault of their own. Other children had feckless and negligent parents, criminally indifferent some, gamblers, heavy drinkers, work-shies, whom I saw regularly in the queue that formed outside the pawnbroker's shop opposite the school every Monday morning. Some children had criminal parents in the legal sense, thieves and housebreakers; one father was a convicted coiner, another operated an illicit still, three at least were brothel- keepers, another was involved in a brutal race-gang knifing near the school which resulted in several murder charges. One family, unable to afford a funeral, buried their dead baby in the back garden. I heard of prostitution, incest, sodomy in our children's homes. One of the boys, from a desperately poor family, was solicited by a wealthy local busines man and cruelly assaulted sexually. Poverty I knew about well enough in Merthyr before I came to Cardiff, but direct contact with the conjunction of poverty, vice and crime was new to me and I found the experience deeply shocking and distressing. When a child in my class was ill I would sometimes go to his house or room after school to see how he was progressing, and what I witnessed on these visits, the squalor, the overcrowding, the degradation, the poverty, I have never forgotten.

from *The Dragon has Two Tongues* (1968)

ALUN LLYWELYN-WILLIAMS

Springtime in the City

I've no recollection at all of the house where I was born. It stood at the foot of Pen-y-Lan hill in the city of Cardiff, but within eighteen months of my birth, the family had moved. My father went away to the war, and my mother took us, the children, to live with my grandmother in Rhyl. At the end of the war, it was once again necessary to seek a home in Cardiff. One was found before long in a house not far from the place where I first opened my eyes on this world and life. Number 33, Ninian Road, Roath Park, was to be my home for the next eighteen years.

Our house was one of a terrace. A fairly large house, nevertheless, with three floors and a cellar, and spacious old-fashioned rooms with prodigally high ceilings. It faced the open park known as the 'recri'. From the front rooms, there was a very pleasant view of the 'recri', and of the wooded slopes of Pen-y-Lan on the far side, and on Saturday afternoon, or on a summer's evening when the park was filled with the activity of sports lovers, it was a lively and colourful scene. But my bedroom was at the back, on the top floor, and from there the view was pretty soulless. The most prominent feature in it was the slate roof of that part of the house which jutted out into the back yard, and the little iron railings above the gutter, intended to prevent the snow falling in destructive lumps onto the greenhouse beneath when the thaw came. Then there was a glimpse of part of the yard itself, or at least of the dark-tiled path which led to the door into the back lane. We called it the 'back-yard', but there was in fact a patch of grass surviving in the guise of a lawn, and untidy leafy tendrils from an orange tree, or so they called it, trailing around an iron archway near the wash-house at the far end. To us as a family, the wash-house was a source of pride. None of our neighbours had anything like it in their gardens, but the great drawback of the wash-house in my eyes was that it restricted even further a patch of ground which was already too small on which to play cricket properly. Quite why we children had to struggle to play cricket in the back yard with the wide acres of the 'recri' so conveniently at hand, I cannot now understand. No-one could address the ball with any enthusiasm without sending it over the wall into next-door, and that was the start of trouble. My sister Enid possessed the amazing talent, amazing even in a girl, for bowling the ball straight over the wall.

It's a pretty colourless view of the world that I remember from my bedroom window. The white flowers of the orange tree and the purple bloom of the Michaelmas daisies in their season: that was the only colour in the garden. On a rockery near the greenhouse grew a dismal cluster of ferns. At the far end of the garden, behind the wash-house, there was a back lane, and there stood a small workshop, part of a timber yard. When I was ill sometimes, and had to stay unwillingly in bed, the plaintive sound of the circular saw would come and comfort me. Around the timber yard, there was nothing to be seen but the grey behinds of the back-street houses, and their roofs, and the tops and roofs and chimneys of the innumerable other streets beyond, with nothing but the occasional office-block or cinema or school, or the spire of an occasional church, rising above the monotony. But far away in the centre of it all rose the white tower of the City Hall. When the wind was in the west, I could hear the clock chiming every quarter hour. And on the horizon on the very edge of the city, there was a line of low hills. They seemed to me to be many miles away. It was years before I ventured into the country beyond those hills.

For most of the year I had the back bedroom to myself, but there were two beds in it, and when my brother came home from school on holiday, he would share the room with me. I was glad to have the company of my brother Eric. Not because I felt lonely — I don't remember feeling lonely at all in our house, although I sometimes felt afraid, afraid of the dark of the landing at night, and afraid of being so far from the cheerfulness of the living room on the ground floor and from the room where my father and mother slept. But my brother was quite a lot older than me, and I greatly admired him because he had the obvious authority of a man of the world. Eric was kind-hearted and was quite prepared to take notice of his younger brother and to entertain him on occasion with lively reports of the antics and valour of his friends and himself at school. He had a particular talent for telling stories, and one of my favourite pastimes was to listen to him sometimes before going to sleep creating exciting fantasies with his own fertile imagination and from the material of an adventure book he'd read recently, perhaps from the work of Rider Haggard, or John Buchan or H.G. Wells. That laid the foundation of a habit which has persisted all my life, never retiring properly until after midnight, and always having something at hand to read before going to sleep.

My sister Enid, like Eric, was at boarding school, and I didn't see much of her. I don't know whether my father had thought of sending me away

71

to school. It was a long time before I went to any sort of school regularly, because when I was four, it was found that there was a disease in the bone of my hand, and the hand had to be kept in a splint for years, and I had to stay at home quietly to prevent the disease spreading. I was eight years old before I could go to school properly, and when at last the chance came, it was to a private school that I went, a school called Highfield which was kept by two old ladies in a house in the same road as ours and within a terrace or two. There I remained for two years, receiving an education of sorts amongst other children of 'respectable' families of the area whose parents wanted to prevent them from mixing with the dubious multitudes who attended the city's elementary schools. I don't have very much recollection of the place by now, but I have often pondered on the quality of education offered there, and the strange craving of some people which remains even today to support this sort of separatist establishment. I wasn't unhappy there and I almost believe, I have to admit, that Highfield was in some things a little ahead for that period. At least I remember the painting lessons, and how we were encouraged, as we practised our painting, not only to copy real paintings as examples, but also to experiment freely with colour and drawing as we wished — the sort of exercise which has found great favour in primary schools since the last war and which has been very fruitful but which was almost unknown in a period when drawing lessons were mainly confined to copying pretty worthless geometric forms.

Whatever the advantages Highfield could boast socially, one thing quickly became clear. I had little hope of ever passing the examination which would earn me a place in the High School from there. And it was on the High School that I had set my sights, mine and my parents'. The High School was a prestigious school, taking pupils from every part of the city, and it was quite an achievement for a boy to be accepted into the ranks of the elect. I was transferred therefore from the private school to the nearest city elementary school, again conveniently near to our house, a huge forbidding building of uncompromising red brick set in the middle of the back streets, where hundreds of children of every shape and colour received their education. I'm eternally grateful for that experience, not so much because of the formal education I received there — that, within limits, was quite acceptable, I suppose — but because of the chance it gave me to mix with a host of boys of my own age for the first time, who taught me that differences of class, background and religion were no hindrance in the world to making lasting friendships. It was a very

72

valuable experience for a boy who had hitherto led a narrow and sheltered life, and I'm glad to say that some of the friends I made in that elementary school have remained loyal to this day. I was a fair scholar but hopeless at arithmetic. I never managed to conquer that weakness, but the teacher, a man this time (thankfully!), a solid and determined man who took his work with each one of us seriously, managed somehow to get me into good enough shape even in arithmetic (temporarily at least) to pass the High School examination at the end of two years. The year that I succeeded in this test, Eric finished at boarding school and came home to start his College course. And soon afterwards, my sister Enid, with her school career also at an end, came home to live while she considered how to earn her living in the world. In the end, she decided to become a nurse, but that meant that she stayed in Cardiff. For a short time, perhaps some three or four years, the family were together in one place.

It's pleasant to be raised in a large town from one point of view — there are always so many interesting things happening and so much to do, and in our home at least, where there was much coming and going, there were so many interesting people to meet. Back in the 'twenties, it is possible that we were more privileged than many. My mother and father, as I can now see, were pretty sensible parents. They didn't interfere *too much* with the children although some of the conventions of the household seemed to us then to be rather restricting and old-fashioned. They were so of course to some extent, and we responded at times with impatience to the gap which inevitably arises between every two generations. My father, I must admit, was something of a puzzle to me at times. Because he was a doctor, and a public figure, and of rather an adventurous spirit, his ideas on some subjects were very advanced, and he gave us complete freedom to choose our own friends, and, within reasonable limits, to find and pursue our own interests as we chose. But he was also, as the son of a poor minister, very aware that he had had to make his own way in the world. Through great sacrifice in the face of many tiresome difficulties he had earned himself an honoured and responsible position, and established a comfortable home for his family. The ideas of Samuel Smiles and the elevated morals of the age of Queen Victoria were never far from his mind, and despite his generosity and natural kindness he could sometimes be stubbornly principled in matters which were not pleasing to us children. Take the chapel for instance. We had to go to every service and meeting in chapel on Sunday, and on week-days too, unless that is we had work to do. Education and school work were more important even than means of grace. By the time I had reached adolescence my brother and sister had eased the way for me in many matters, and had won the occasional battle for freedom. I was the child of his middle age — my father was forty-three when I was born, and strangely enough, within the following year, he had packed his bag and joined the army, and recruited there his own Sanitary Section, and had gone to the war, where he won the Military Cross for his bravery, and several other honours from a grateful French Government for special services to its soldiers and civilians. Goodness knows why he insisted on going to the war at his age — he didn't have to. But I suppose he was a man who liked to accept a challenge, and once he had decided on some course or on the justice of some issue, he couldn't be moved. And he would take the thing to extremes. He was, of course, a great temperance man, but in my father's eyes, temperance meant total abstinence. And yet, no-one was ever less of a tyrant than he was. . . .

I don't know how much sympathy my mother had with my father's religious interests. She was, of course, completely loyal to him, and always tolerated everything he did, not only, I suspect, because that was the behaviour expected of a woman brought up on the Victorian ideal, but also because she obviously adored her husband, and remained to her grave as much in love with him as she always had been, and he with her. And yet I sense that she couldn't always have been of the same opinion as him in religious matters. I never saw her apply herself with enthusiasm to chapel activities, and she wasn't either as I remember too regular in her attendance. It was strange the number of times a headache or a sudden touch of a cold would keep her away, and we children would have to struggle to chapel without her, secretly envious of her indisposition. She seldom went to week-day meetings. And at times she would give us some indication of her disapproval of some aspects of religious behaviour which she considered to be extreme, such as revivals. The 1904 revival had in her experience carried things too far. She considered the uncontrolled feelings observed in a revival to be unseemly, and not the way responsible Christians should behave publicly, because they could lead to uncivilized and immoral behaviour. My father made nothing of such dangers. And a rather unfortunate thing occurred when the revivalist himself, Evan Roberts, reappeared from somewhere, after years of silence, with the intention, it was said, of re-kindling the fire. He took the service in our chapel one evening, and although he did not, I'm afraid, carry much conviction, the occasion was a strange experience to many and an unhappy frustration to some. But my father was delighted. He insisted on inviting Evan Roberts to our house, and, worse, to the horror of us all, he also insisted on persuading him to pray on our behalf in the large front room, the family and maid and guests kneeling uncomfortably self-conscious each by his own easy chair. For a moment, I caught my mother's eye. I'll never forget her expression, half mischievous and half in mute protest against such unseemly behaviour in her own best parlour. . . .

My father never tried to persuade me to become a doctor. In two things only did I feel the effect of his strong hand in my upbringing. One of those was the chapel, and since I didn't go away to school as my brother and sister did, I had more than my share of chapel. Chapel-going became a burden to me, and I don't believe that I received much benefit to my soul from over attendance at services. I hated having to say my verse, and hated even more, when I grew older, receiving a summons to take part in the young people's prayer-meeting. At one stage there were five services every Sunday in our chapel, and my father was partly to blame for that, because he, as one of the hard-working elders, was responsible for establishing the young people's prayer-meeting before the morning service. This early morning prayer-meeting was a great tribulation to me. I must admit that I was, like many growing boys I suppose, rather reluctant to get out of bed on Sunday morning, and to shake myself prematurely from the luxurious void of the *capel gwyn* (the 'white chapel') — as I recently heard it referred to by a younger generation — to partake in a privilege I treated with some suspicion, went very much against the grain. . . .

There was no sense, as I saw it, in having to go to five services every Sunday. My father never went to Sunday School or to the Singing School, nor my mother, and I considered that to be unfair. But there was a pleasurable side to things. For one thing there was the company of the boys, and of the girls for that matter, in the Sunday School. And in connection with the Sunday School, there was of course the annual outing. In those days, the Heol-y-Crwys chapel would usually hire a field at Whitsun on farm-land somewhere on the outskirts of the city, in Rhiwbina or Rumney, and spending a whole day in the countryside playing and taking part in organized sports was a rare and absorbing experience for most of us city children. In fact we preferred a trip to the country like this to a day at the seaside in Barry or Porthcawl, because our mode of transport out into the country was much more exciting than a journey in a charabanc or on the train. One of the elders owned a coal business, and this talented and humorous man, known to all as *John Williams y glo* ('the coal') would put his coal-carts at the disposal of the Sunday School — scrubbed clean beforehand of course, although it was too much to expect them to be totally free of the remains of the black dust. On these carts were placed benches from the vestry, lashed down tightly and safely so that the passengers could sit comparatively free from care and observe the world around them from an elevated height. And the carts were no ordinary unromantic lorries. They were drawn by horses. And such horses! Large heavy muscular horses, their harnesses on that day gleaming in splendour, and their brass adornments and coloured ribbons a wonder to all who beheld them. To be carried through the ordinary traffic in an old-fashioned cart behind these colourful and impressive horses was a joyful experience. It's true that our progress through the streets was slow, but all the better for that. There was more chance of us being seen in all our glory, and for other less fortunate children to admire and envy us. Certainly a trip like this was the highlight of the Sunday School year.

I hadn't much to say of the School itself. Like R.T. Jenkins, I'm afraid that I benefited little from it, with one exception, and that exception is rather an important one. For one period, when I was around thirteen years old, we had a remarkable teacher in the class of which I was a member, a woman named Mrs Isaac, who came to Cardiff, with her husband and family, from Aberdare. She wasn't, as far as I know, a trained teacher, but she was a natural teacher of unusual talent, who took great care in preparing her lessons and who knew instinctively how to make them interesting to children. I remember her with gratitude, not only nor primarily because of her guidance in the Sunday School class but also for her interest in the class members outside the School, in our general culture. I'm almost certain that it was Mrs Isaac who first took me to the theatre — my father and mother weren't active theatregoers, although they surely weren't in favour of the frightening insinuation I saw in our family copy of that strange book *Y Gwr Ieuanc Oddicartref* that the playhouse was the broad road and open gateway which led to destruction. Indeed my father once took me to see *Journey's End* in London, probably because it was to do with the war. But every now and then, Mrs Isaac would arrange to take her Sunday School class together to the theatre. That was, I remember, how I first saw a performance of *The Merchant of Venice* in the New Theatre. Certainly I and the other children are very much indebted to this intelligent teacher, although my education in the

76

day school of course opened the same doors to me. Mrs Isaac's great favour to me was to show that chapel and religion did not have to be incompatible with culture and the arts. For that matter, she wasn't the only one, even in chapel, to attempt to promote the general culture of the children and young people. I remember our minister, the Reverend William Davies, *Bugail y Crwys* ('the Shepherd of Crwys') as he was affectionately known by everyone in Cardiff, once tried to instruct some of us in the *cynganeddion*. William Davies came originally from Cwm Ystwyth. He worked in the coal mines for a time before he was called to the ministry and was able to go to College. A kind and liberal-minded man after my own heart because he was fond of poetry and of rugby football. He was a good Welsh scholar, and I believe he had held classes on Welsh language and literature in the church before this, because one of my literary treasures is a small pamphlet entitled *Gramadeg, Cynghanedd, Canu Penillion* which he had published as far back as 1916 and which I came across by accident in John Evans's old shop. In the class of which I became a member, William Davies was aided by Ceindeg Humphreys, the eldest daughter of the senior elder, Evan Humphreys, who had, at the time, just finished her college course and was an excellent Welsh scholar. I don't know how long the class carried on or how successful it was — it couldn't have been a great success in my case because I've no recollection at all of what we learned there, and I never grasped the *cynganeddion* properly, even when it became mandatory in a few years time to have some idea of the rules of *Cerdd Dafod*. Probably I was far too young to appreciate my old minister's endeavour and to take advantage of it, but it seems to me today that he did a very unusual thing in a chapel in his period. And I believe that I enjoyed the class. It was, certainly, more entertaining than the *seiat* (the Fellowship meeting).

The truth is that in the chapel there was a close, warm and kind community, and that was what mattered to me, not the religious aspect. Or at least, the creeds and theologizing and moralising we heard there didn't touch me, and it didn't cross my mind at the time that religion could have anything to do with the nature of the community. When I came in time to read Caradoc Evans's attacks on the Nonconformist community, the satire was completely unintelligible to me. Although so much connected with chapel was unacceptable to me, my memories of the characters in the community I knew are happy and bright. There was humanity there, and if I had to suffer much boredom, I was also able to experience much brotherly love. There was as well a funny side. It was a great delight, for instance, to slide to the far end of our pew (where I often sat alone) and feel the hand of the woman who sat immediately behind me reaching stealthily over the back of the pew with a fistful of cigarette-cards. She was the wife of an elder and had two grown-up sons, and they and the husband must have smoked like furnaces, because hardly a Sabbath passed that I did not receive a substantial pile of these cards. Glancing at the cards during the sermon was a priceless help in passing the time, but I soon learned, I'm ashamed to admit, that there were other means, just as pleasant, of entertaining myself. How easy it was to slip quietly into a daydream and imagine myself to be some adventurous hero I'd seen in the cinema the week before, perhaps Douglas Fairbanks in *The Black Pirate*, and imagine I was, like him, leaping nimbly from spar to spar on the enemy ship, performing similar acrobatics on the beams of the chapel ceiling to the immense astonishment of the saints. I would descend victoriously into the *Sêt Fawr* (elders' pew) where Mari, the precentor's beautiful daughter, had been cruelly bound to the side of the pulpit, and would rescue her masterfully from the elders' clutches. The feat of course was to yield to these escapist delights and give the impression at the same time that you were listening intently to every word of the sermon. I was remarkably successful in this, and never considered myself at the time to be a consummate hypocrite. . . .

I'm afraid that the circumstances of our lives were too difficult for years for my father's efforts with the Welsh language. Naturally I, like lads and youths of every age, reacted instinctively against the ideals of the older generation, and amongst those ideals the loyalty to the language appeared to be particularly pointless and unreasonable. After all, I was growing up in a world very different from the age which decided the whole way of thinking of my parents, and my interests were inevitably foreign to them, at every level. My father never had the opportunity when he was a lad of following the successes and catastrophes of the unpredictable Glamorgan cricket team, and the names of my idols in that field, Bates and Bell and N.V.H. Riches and Mercer and Ryan, meant nothing to him. He never had the chance of watching the excitements of rugby playing at Cardiff Arms Park, not to mention the ecstasy of playing the game itself, and he never had the chance to go to the pictures, nor to waste his time with that wonderful new gadget, the crystal set. These were the sorts of things which filled my mind, and wandering with my friends to search out the delights of the city, down to the docks to watch the ships being loaded and unloaded and venture guardedly to the centre of the unknown but attractive dangers of Tiger Bay; or simply to wander the main streets and admire the great public buildings and splendid parks. I was proud of the city of Cardiff. I believed it to be the most beautiful and most interesting city in the world, and I dreamed of ways of making it even better and more beautiful and elevating its status. I was sorry that the excellent Museum building had not yet been completed, and I tried to imagine it finished in the future. I suspect that some of these feelings at least were not entirely strange to my father. He would show me a piece of land in Cathays Park every now and then and tell me that on that site he expected to see the buildings of a Parliament House for Wales some day. But those were rare occasions when I had a glimpse like this that there could after all be a means of communication and understanding between father and son. To every appearance, he hadn't much sympathy with my general interests, nor with my dreams, nor any interest in my early literary efforts. On the other hand I regretted his oldfashioned narrowmindedness, and his zeal for religion and temperance and his strange stubbornness about the Welsh language. There was a gap between us, undoubtedly, and at the time I accepted that without complaint and without question. . . .

It took a very long time for my father and me to close that gap and establish the close and living relationship between us we had desired so long. It's good to think that we succeeded nobly in the end, after I had grown to be enough of a man to understand and respect his viewpoint without necessarily accepting it myself and come to appreciate fully all that he did for us children in his great love for us.

translated by Luned Meredith from *Gwanwyn yn y Ddinas* (1975)

ROALD DAHL

The Bicycle and the Sweet-shop

When I was seven, my mother decided I should leave kindergarten and go to a proper boys' school. By good fortune, there existed a well-known Preparatory School for boys about a mile from our house. It was called Llandaff Cathedral School, and it stood right under the shadow of Llandaff Cathedral. Like the cathedral, the school is still there and still flourishing.

But here again, I can remember very little about the two years I attended Llandaff Cathedral School, between the age of seven and nine. Only two moments remain clearly in my mind. The first lasted not more than five seconds but I will never forget it.

It was my first term and I was walking home alone across the village green after school when suddenly one of the senior twelve-year-old boys came riding full speed down the road on his bicycle about twenty yards away from me. The road was on a hill and the boy was going down the slope, and as he flashed by he started backpedalling very quickly so that the free-wheeling mechanism of his bike made a loud whirring sound. At the same time, he took his hands off the handlebars and folded them casually across his chest. I stopped dead and stared after him. How wonderful he was! How swift and brave and graceful in his long trousers with bicycle-clips around them and his scarlet school cap at a jaunty angle on his head! One day, I told myself, one glorious day I will have a bike like that and I will wear long trousers with bicycle-clips and my school cap will sit jaunty on my head and I will go whizzing down the hill pedalling backwards with no hands on the handlebars!

I promise you that if somebody had caught me by the shoulder at that moment and said to me, "What is your greatest wish in life, little boy? What is your absolute ambition? To be a doctor? A fine musician? A painter? A writer? Or the Lord Chancellor?" I would have answered without hesitation that my only ambition, my hope, my longing was to have a bike like that and to go whizzing down the hill with no hands on the handlebars. It would be fabulous. It made me tremble just to think about it.

My second and only other memory of Llandaff Cathedral School is extremely bizarre. It happened a little over a year later, when I was just nine. By then I had made some friends and when I walked to school in the mornings I would start out alone but would pick up four other boys of my own age along the way. After school was over, the same four boys and I would set out together across the village green and through the village itself, heading for home. On the way to school and on the way back we always passed the sweet-shop. No we didn't, we never passed it. We always stopped. We lingered outside its rather small window gazing in at the big glass jars full of Bull's-eyes and Old Fashioned Humbugs and Strawberry Bonbons and Glacier Mints and Acid Drops and Pear Drops and Lemon Drops and all the rest of them. Each of us received sixpence a week for pocket-money, and whenever there was any money in our pockets, we would all troop in together to buy a pennyworth of this or that. My own favourites were Sherbet Suckers and Liquorice Bootlaces.

One of the other boys, whose name was Thwaites, told me I should never eat Liquorice Bootlaces. Thwaites's father, who was a doctor, had said that they were made from rats' blood. The father had given his young son a lecture about Liquorice Bootlaces when he had caught him eating one in bed. "Every ratcatcher in the country", the father had said, "takes his rats to the Liquorice Bootlace Factory, and the manager pays tuppence for each rat. Many a ratcatcher has become a millionaire by selling his dead rats to the Factory."

"But how do they turn the rats into liquorice?" the young Thwaites had asked his father.

"They wait until they've got ten thousand rats," the father had answered, "then they dump them all into a huge shiny steel cauldron and boil them up for several hours. Two men stir the bubbling cauldron with long poles and in the end they have a thick steamy rat-stew. After that, a cruncher is lowered into the cauldron to crunch the bones, and what's left is a pulpy substance called rat-mash."

"Yes, but how do they turn that into Liquorice Bootlaces, Daddy?" the young Thwaites had asked, and this question, according to Thwaites, had caused his father to pause and think for a few moments before he answered it. At last he had said, "The two men who were doing the stirring with the long poles now put on their wellington boots and climb into the cauldron and shovel the hot rat-mash out on to a concrete floor. Then they run a steam-roller over it several times to flatten it out. What is left looks rather like a gigantic black pancake, and all they have to do after that is to wait for it to cool and to harden so that they can cut it up into strips and make the Bootlaces. Don't ever eat them," the father had said. "If you do you'll get ratitis."

"What is ratitis, Daddy?" young Thwaites had asked.

"All the rats that the rat-catchers catch are poisoned with rat-poison," the father had said. "It's the rat-poison that gives you ratitis."

"Yes, but what happens to you when you catch it?" young Thwaites had asked.

"Your teeth become very sharp and pointed," the father had answered. "And a short stumpy tail grows out of your back just above your bottom. There is no cure for ratitis. I ought to know. I'm a doctor."

We all enjoyed Thwaites's story and we made him tell it to us many times on our walks to and from school. But it didn't stop any of us, except Thwaites, from buying Liquorice Bootlaces. At two for a penny they were the best value in the shop.

from *Boy* (1984)

IORWERTH C. PEATE

The Garden Village

When I went there at the end of March 1927, Cardiff was a city unfamiliar to me. I had been there for a brief afternoon, to receive my degree, in July 1921 and for another brief afternoon in July 1926, for the interview that was mentioned in the preceding chapter. So that March, my Morris-Cowley carried me, with my father's tool-chest full of my books in the back of the vehicle, to a city that I did not know, and to a district that was to be a new home for me for half a century. My friend Arthur ap Gwynn, my old teacher's son, had very kindly invited me to lodge with him in Connaught Road, a quiet road within easy reach of the Museum. Arthur and I were co-lodgers (changing our lodgings twice) for more than two years, until my marriage in September 1929: he went soon afterwards to become head librarian of the University College at Aberystwyth. There was never a cross word between us and indeed one could not have wished for a better or truer friend.

There was no obvious Welsh life of any kind in the city at that time, and I longed greatly for the community of my native patch in Montgomeryshire and for the jolly company of my old classes in Cardiganshire and Merioneth. I escaped as often as possible to the town of Rhymney where my fiancée, by then, was a Welsh teacher in the grammar school, and I came to appreciate the close, warm community of the Welsh working-class in that part of Monmouthshire.

On the first Sunday evening in Cardiff, I went to Ebenezer chapel to listen to a sermon by Dr H.M. Hughes. I knew no one there but by some miracle Dr Morgan Watkin, a prominent Baptist and Professor of French in the University College, was there and he recognised me. At the close of the service he took me to his home for supper and a chat. I shall never forget the kindness of that gracious gentleman who remained a dear friend of mine until his death. When I went the following morning to the Museum the place was humming with unusual activity. They were preparing for the official opening of the Museum by King George V at the end of April. They had no time to waste on a newcomer like me and I spent the day wandering around the building, rather glum and somehow half-wondering whether I had made a terrible mistake in coming to such a place. My doubts grew when I discovered that there was not a single

Welsh-speaking Welshman among the entire staff. But eventually I discovered, in her office on the Museum's top floor, one Welsh woman, namely Miss Edith Breese who was the institution's librarian. She was a relation of Mynyddog's and belonged to the Breese family of Cyfeiliog. If I was glad to make her acquaintance, she rejoiced that there was by now one Welshman on the staff and many were my visits to the library for the sake of a chat in our own language. Apart from members of the Department in which I was to work only one man came to welcome me and to offer his help and advice should I find myself in difficulty. That was Harold A. Hyde, Keeper of the Botany Department, a native of Ipswich, a devotional Christian and a man who gave me the privilege of his friendship throughout my years in the National Museum.

At about the time I moved from Aberystwyth to Cardiff, there appeared in *Y Faner* a review of mine of the second edition of *Ynys yr Hud a Chaneuon Eraill* and soon after I had begun my work in the Museum I received a letter from Professor W.J. Gruffydd thanking me for the review and inviting me to his house in Lôn-y-Dail, Rhiwbina, for a chat and tea on the following Sunday afternoon. I had never seen Gruffydd let alone met him, and after hearing so much from various people about his 'ferocity' and his 'critical tendency' I felt quite humble, not to say apprehensive, as I went to Lôn-y-Dail that Sunday afternoon. But I soon saw that there was no basis whatsoever to the insinuations I had heard. Gruffydd and his wife, Gwenda, were really welcoming and we had hours of pleasant conversation. It was obvious that what I had written in *Y Faner* had pleased him and he put great emphasis, on that occasion and many others, on the fact that I "understood him", indeed this expression almost became some kind of 'magic word' between us. Anyway, he put extraordinary store on people who 'understood him' and he accepted them, warts and all. The ones he rejected were those whom he often described as "a decent old boy *but* . . .".

Gruffydd's next-door neighbour was R.T. Jenkins and Gruffydd was a kind patron of his throughout his time in Cardiff. Because of the impediment in his speech, R.T. was advanced in years before he started to take a part in Welsh public life. That is why, perhaps, R.T. became in his middle age so fond of committee-work and conferences. And Gruffydd succeeded in persuading him to begin writing in Welsh. Indeed, it was by his contributions to *Y Llenor* that R.T. Jenkins established himself as a Welsh writer. Those who have read *Edrych yn Ol* by R.T. Jenkins will doubtless have noticed what he said about "the most comfortable, most beautiful — dearest indeed is the right word — little house that I was ever in". That was 24 Lôn-y- Dail, "next door to W.J. Gruffydd".

The 'garden village' in Rhiwbina was a co-operative venture which bore the prosaic name 'The Cardiff Workers' Co-operative Garden Village'. It was started before the First World War by men like Sir Daniel Lleufer Thomas, Professor Stanley Jevons, Professor W.J. Gruffydd and others. Gruffydd was responsible for the Welsh names — Lôn-y-Dail, Lôn Isa, Pen-y-Dre and Y Groes — and a fine architect by the name of Mottram (a brother if I remember rightly of R.H. Mottram, the English writer) designed the houses. Later on he was followed by T. Alwyn Lloyd. Care was taken that there were gardens and lawns around every house — you will remember that W.J. Gruffydd wrote in 1917 in Port Saiud about "the house between gardens on the outskirts of Cardiff town". Everyone who took a house there was asked to buy a number of shares in the Society — fifty pounds was the minimum when I went there — and he received an annual interest on the sum and security of tenure for life if he so wished, as long as he paid the (very reasonable) rent regularly and kept his house in order. A man on the spot looked after all the houses. The whole was run by a committee of the tenants, which was presided over by each member of the committee in turn. On occasions we had extraordinary fun in the meetings of this committee, as when the village policeman retired and the committee gave him a generous gift in recognition of the duties he had *not* carried out! My wife and I took a home in Lôn-y-Dail in 1929 and we stayed there for nineteen years. When we went there R.T. Jenkins and W.J. Gruffydd were living almost opposite us. W. Hughes Jones (*Elidir Sais*) was in the same street during his much too brief sojourn with the BBC, and in 1936 my friend and colleague Ffransis Payne arrived. In Lôn-y- Dail there also lived Professor Cyril Brett, the English Professor at University College, D. Gwilym James, a fellow-student of mine at Aberystwyth who later became Vice-Chancellor and Principal of Southampton University, and Gwyn Jones, who was the Professor of English at University College, Cardiff. until his retirement in 1975. There too was W.S. Purchon, head of the Architecture Department in the Technical College (as it was then). To Lôn Isa came Professor David Williams (later of Aberystwyth), John Griffiths of the BBC and Morris Williams and his wife Dr Kate Roberts before they moved to the Rhondda and thence to look after *Y Faner* in Denbigh. In Heol-y- Deri lived John Llewelyn Williams, editor of *Gwaith Guto'r Glyn*, and beyond the stream was the home of D. Llywelyn Walters and his wife Olwen.

When Tom Bassett, the publisher of *Y Llenor* at the *Hughes a'i Fab* Press in Wrexham, moved to the office in Cardiff he became a neighbour of ours in the house next door on the corner of Lôn Isa and Lôn-y-Dail. It was a pleasure to hear him speaking Pentyrch Welsh. He had been a prisoner in Dartmoor during the First World War, but was reluctant to say much about what he had suffered there for his principles. Heol-wen was a new street where about four or five houses had been built which belonged to their occupants. There lived T. Alwyn Lloyd, the architect, Professor Grundy, the Professor of Latin at University College, Harold A. Hyde to whom I have already referred, Keeper of the Botany Department in the National Museum, Sir Cyril Fox, the Museum's Director, and Edward Lewis, the mild-mannered solicitor from Maesycymer who was friend and adviser to us all.

So, although we lived in a district that was not Welsh in language, our community was a strong and interesting one. For years several of us travelled back and forth to our work on the little train that ran from Queen Street station in Cardiff through the Heath and Rhiwbina as far as Whitchurch. At Rhiwbina David, the elder brother of the Right Honourable Clement Davies, leader of the Liberal Party for a while, joined us and often in his bowler-hat he used to carry small posies of flowers from his garden that he distributed during the journey to town among the ladies who travelled daily with us. At the Heath, John Davies (from Betws-yn-Rhos) joined the company, on his way to the City Library to work on his numerous essays and his *magnum opus*, *Bywyd a Gwaith Moses Williams* (Cardiff, 1937). There were so many Welsh-speaking people living in the village that Professor Gruffydd, who was no more than most of us a keen chapel-goer, was prompted to start a weekly Sunday School and a monthly sermon in the comparatively small hall that stood near Lôn-y-Dail.

translated by Meic Stephens from *Rhwng Dau Fyd* (1976)

GLYN JONES

The Common Path

On one side the hedge, on the other the brook:
Each afternoon I passed, unnoticed,
The middle-aged schoolmistress, grey-haired,
Gay, loving, who went home along the path.

That spring she walked briskly, carrying her bag
With the long ledger, the ruler, the catkin twigs,
Two excited little girls from her class
Chattering around their smiling teacher.

Summer returned, each day then she approached slowly,
Alone, wholly absorbed, as though in defeat
Between water and hazels, her eyes heedless,
Her grey face deeply cast down. Could it be
Grief at the great universal agony had begun
To feed upon her heart — war, imbecility,
Old age, starving, children's deaths, deformities?
I, free, white, gentile, born neither
Dwarf nor idiot, passed her by, drawing in
The skirts of my satisfaction, on the other side.

One day, at the last instant of our passing,
She became, suddenly, aware of me
And, as her withdrawn glance met my eyes,
Her whole face kindled into life, I heard
From large brown eyes a blare of terror, anguished
Supplication, her cry of doom, death, despair.
And in the warmth of that path's sunshine
And of my small and manageable success
I felt at once repelled, affronted by her suffering,
The naked shamelessness of that wild despair.

Troubled, I avoided the common until I heard
Soon, very soon, the schoolmistress, not from

Any agony of remote and universal suffering
   Or unendurable grief for others, but
Private, middle-aged, rectal cancer, was dead.

What I remember, and in twenty years have
   Never expiated, is that my impatience,
That one glance of my intolerance,
   Rejected her, and so rejected all
The sufferings of wars, imprisonments,
   Deformities, starvation, idiocy, old age —
Because fortune, sunlight, meaningless success,
   Comforted an instant what must not be comforted.

GWYN JONES

Come on, Wales!

They spent half an hour over their lunch, and then, at Shelton's suggestion, left early for the Park. "I like the feel of a gathering crowd," he said. They were on the ground half an hour before the start, and Shelton hoped Brimble was already in, for they would be closing the gates soon. The crowd was by no means still. Where the gangways came up on the popular side there was a constant movement and change, and occasionally, to the accompaniment of screams and shouts they saw the remarkable and perilous swaying that characterised Cardiff Arms Park at that time. There were not enough barriers, the crowd was not sufficiently divided, and as a result there were directions of pressure ending in between two hundred and a thousand spectators losing all control of their feet and weight. If you were in one, you suddenly felt a flooding of bodies at your back, tried to brace yourself, felt your feet leave the terracing, and away you went, sometimes completely off the ground, sometimes at a sort of running stumble, in a dreadful, helpless lurch. "Whoops!" the swayers cried, and "There she goes!" came from the excited onlookers. When at last the sway had spent itself upon broad backs or the railings in front, there was a lesser progress backwards, and then settlement again. "They should be able to stop that," said Broddam, and explained to Mrs Shelton how such swayings occurred. "How dreadful!" she exclaimed. Above the heads of the mass floated a light blue fringe of tobacco smoke. Then they started singing, desultorily, keeping different times in different parts of the ground, to a tune different from that the band was playing. An old white-headed man waving a stout stick ran out from the ringside seats, and began to conduct with great sweeping strokes. First one group, then another, joined in, made contact, surrendered themselves, and forty thousand voices in one mighty choir sent 'Cwm Rhondda' pouring through the restless air. Some were singing in English, some in Welsh; chapel, church, and disbelievers — "Bread of Heaven, Bread of Heaven, Feed me till I want no more — Feed me till I want no more." They sang like men who find heartsease in singing, sustained and chant-like. More than two thirds there were from the hills and valleys, and in their voices one felt the austerity of toil, the passion of mountains under the stars, the sadness and grinding of their crude livelihood. The tune was changed.

'Jesu, Lover of my Soul' — whitehead announced in a high, lilting voice, and the regimental band was with him. Louise, prepared to scoff, grew still and tense. Much that she had found in this people — its meanness, ugliness of life, and oftentimes savage hypocrisy — for the time she forgot, at the stupendous outpouring of this cry of sorrow for the New Jerusalem. The hymn died away like a universal supplication — and then came comedy. The next song dissipated religion and tears together. 'Sospan Fach,' cried whitehead, and only half the band could play for him. The gates had been shut long before this, and the kick-off was near. When they sang the Welsh national anthem, all those sitting in the stand rose, and most took off their hats. Louise rather resented this. It was like standing for the Marseillaise or something equally foreign. Yet, when the words had been twice sung, there were tears in her eyes. The ocean-swell of sound flooded the sky, poured into the thin blue, and was oddly over. Then it was time to start.

The Scots came on first, generously, even uproariously greeted, and then came the glorious scarlet of the home team. This was rapture.

"There must be a couple of hundred from the Cwm here to-day," Shelton told his wife.

Personalities were pointed out. Carbright — fastest man in the game; Fisher — standing by the gaunt forward — Bob Llewellyn — best forward playing to-day; MacAndrew and Burns, their halves; Seaforth and Tom Rees, the backs. The whistle blew. Gaels and Celts combined to sing the national anthem, and then the game started, Scotland playing from the river end. Without much success Louise tried to follow her husband's explanations. She heard that Scotland had scored after ten minutes and again after half an hour, but what she really enjoyed was the way the two packs set at each other towards the end of the first half. It needed no technical knowledge to appreciate this elemental matching of strong men. Patricians are never slow to turn down their thumbs. Skuse, that mighty blacksmith's helper, came staggering through in front of the stand, three men clinging around his neck and waist. She saw his chest heave up and out, and then he crashed like a tree, dragging his parasites with him. They all wriggled clear, and he scrambled up, his jersey in ribbons. Off it came, and there was the bulk of the man, his back light brown, with red blotches from the scrummages, his barndoor chest clotted with black hair. As his arms went up into the sleeves of his new jersey, there was a rolling of muscles throughout his torso, a rippling of elastic and steel. Bulges came out across his round ribs, a pattern of power and drive. "Shouldn't care to stop him!" Shelton grunted. "By gad, no!" echoed a stranger next to him. For the present Skuse was Shelton and the stranger; they were Skuse. So the hammering went on. Minutes wore themselves to tatters, and play had finally settled in the Scottish twenty-five. A long, muttering roar played over the banks and stands. There was a scrum down under the posts, MacAndrew put the ball in, it came out slowly on the Scottish side, held in the back row, Llewellyn broke away from the scrum, threw himself at MacAndrew as he gathered the ball, it bounced back awkwardly, Shand snapped it up and drop-kicked as he was sent sprawling. The ball hit an upright, there was a groan, bounced on to the crossbar in a deathly silence, and fell over for four points amidst a howl of triumph.

"Eight-four," Shelton explained. "Shand dropped a goal — that's four points." He saw with delight that his wife was adding her handclap to the applause.

There was no further score before half-time.

The second half was desperately hard. Laughter, groans, chatter, cheers, objurgations, some drinking from bottles brought into the ground, and several horrible swayings, showed that the crowd was on its toes. "Come on, Wales!" Louise heard a clear tenor voice shouting from behind the Scottish line: "You'm playing towards the pubs, ain't u?" There were stoppages. "Man out!" Rees had crash-tackled Magraw. A little man in a cloth cap ran on with a sponge, the water dripping as he ran, but before he reached the place of combat Magraw was up, shaking his big head. "Gertcher!" jeered the crowd, and the little man ran back again, with his hand held high. The forwards played murderously — one moment bearing down with the inhuman pressure of a steam-roller, the next, disintegrated, crashing and sprawling. Louise found herself looking for Ben, and cried sharply as he came through the centre, slick as a slice of fat bacon, was forced sideways, and finally hurled winded into touch. They rubbed his belly, shoved his head between his knees, he shook himself like a dog, and the game went on. Six minutes to go. The game settled on the Scottish line. A good touchfinder carried play back to the twenty-five. Three minutes to go. Shand took a long line out. The players seemed to have straggled halfway across the field. Llewellyn jumped up as though he would tear down Olympus, grabbed the ball, and flung it back. Wretchedly it was kicked ahead to Burns, who sliced his kick away to the right. For a moment no one seemed interested in the ball, all the players seemed to be standing still, and then the ground was pandemonium. A figure in a scarlet jersey was coming from nowhere at the ball. It was

Fisher. "By Great God Almighty," someone yelled behind Louise, "he's going to get it!" Seaforth, too, ran for the ball, and the most knowing held their breath as they saw that he was going to fly kick. As his boot drove forward, Ben dived for the ball, insanely, got his hands to it, missing death or injury by an inch. His body was flung across Seaforth's knees, and the full back went down with a screech. But Ben was up, running with his head back, like the madman he was. He saw Burns in front of him, checked himself, stumbled almost on one knee, cleared him in a queer, doubled-over fashion, pulled himself upright, and then, as Magraw caught him by the thighs and Johnson by the head, threw the ball hard and true inside him to Shand, who took the ball on his chest and was over the line for a try under four forwards. Three men were out at once — Fisher, Shand, and Seaforth with a twisted knee — but it was a try. You could hear the row all over the town. Strangers hit strangers' hats off. Men punched each other for joy. No one was sitting down; there had been an unparalleled lurch towards the one corner, and dozens of spectators were overcome by the pressure. It was almost an anticlimax when Tom Rees and Llewellyn arranged the ball as carefully as if it were a big diamond, and Tom, deaf to the crowd, inhumanly cool, took his short run and deftly kicked the two points that brought the score to nine-eight and a victory for Wales.

"We've won!" cried Shelton, on his feet like the rest.

"I'm so glad!" said Louise, who had forgotten with her husband that they were English.

As they waited to leave the stand, Shelton heard Sir Hugh's advice again. "You go to the Park and cheer your head off, if you want to, and then go back to the Cwm like a sensible fellow and see if you can't knock sixpence off Fisher's payroll."

Ben was shaking Shand by the hand. "I knew all through the game, see, me and you, Shand, would get that there try. As for the silly bucker as tried to kick my face in —".

He knew that Lily had seen the game, though not with Snooker, who was there with the rest of the boys. Lily, like Louise, had a ticket for the stand.

from *Times Like These* (1936)

ALUN REES

Cardiff Arms Park

Only to hear some sixty thousand Welshmen
sing natural three-part harmony unrehearsed
while rugby giants battle on the field
is knowing that these men were never English.
The language changes, but the hearts do not.

To see red-jerseyed forwards lift themselves
and drive the startled Englishmen before them
as sixty thousand roar the anthem out
is seeing that this race was never conquered.
The valleys darken, but the fire lives.

To see this, all the same, is to regret
that sixty thousand with this splendid fire
urge fifteen on to drive the English back.
If only they would urge themselves like that.

IDRIS DAVIES

Dawn

In Cardiff at dawn the sky is moist and grey
And the baronets wake from dreams of commerce,
With commercial Spanish grammar on their tongues;
And the west wind blows from the sorrowful seas,
Carrying Brazilian and French and Egyptian orders,
Echoing the accents of commercial success,
And shaking the tugs in the quay.
Puff, little engine, to the valleys at daybreak,
To northward and westward with a voice in the dawn,
And shout to the people that prosperity's coming,
And that coal can be changed into ingots of gold,
And that Cardiff shall be famous when the sun goes down.

EMYR HUMPHREYS

It's What You Call Provincial

Amy was relieved to get past him and lose herself in the urgent movement of people on the pavements of one of the main thoroughfares of the city. The noise and bustle were stimulating. As she hurried along she caught a sound of human voices rising above the traffic: it was as inappropriate as if larks had suddenly burst out singing. The human melody blossomed out of the metallic roar of the traffic, and the people jostling on the pavement seemed pleased enough to hear it. At the entrance to a shopping arcade Amy stopped to watch four unemployed miners singing in the gutter. They were giving themselves wholeheartedly to the music. Under their ragged caps their eyes were closed and their arms and hands were extended in stylised gestures acquired from the concert platform. They moved slowly along as they sang, passing the display windows of a furniture shop without looking at their own reflections in the plate glass. They seemed pleased with the excuse the music gave them for keeping their eyes closed. A paper-seller at his pitch under the arch that marked the entrance to the arcade began to shout out his wares. Amy looked at him resentfully but he ignored her disapproval. She stood still on the edge of the pavement watching the singers' approach. Her limbs seemed paralysed by the plangent sadness of the tune. The words were traditional: it was the tune and the way they sang in doleful harmony that expressed their plight. Fumbling in her handbag she extracted a sixpence and dropped it in the mug that was held out by the oldest miner. She listened fascinated as the quartet in their mufflers and long shabby coats glided down the road like blind men guided by the kerb. She felt a strong hand squeeze her arm and looked up in fright. Pen Lewis was smiling at her.

"Pen! I'm sorry. Am I late?"

"What are you doing? Sleep-walking or street-walking?"

She stared after the singing miners. Many well dressed people were hurrying past them now averting their eyes, as if they had come too close to a source of infection.

"Oh, just look at them," Amy said. "Isn't it terrible?"

Pen drew her past the paper seller into the bright arcade.

"We'll make them pay for that," he said.

95

There was grim determination in his voice.

"And it won't be pennies in a hat, either."

As they walked between the dainty displays in the arcade windows Pen unburdened himself.

"All these fancy buildings," he said. "Very charming, I'm sure. But do you think the snooty buggers will ever admit it was all built out of our sweat and blood? Every single bloody stone. Not on your life, Miss Parry. It's run by fat little Tories of doubtful origins and they fall over themselves to get their names on the Honours List. Just think of them handing out the freedom of the city to an enemy of the working class like Stanley Baldwin. If there's anybody entitled to the freedom of this city it's the miner who created it."

They stood outside the Elaine Restaurant. Pen's voice echoed in the arcade. Heads were turned nervously at the sound of his loud confident voice. Amy looked through the glass at the interior of the restaurant.

"There's a table," she said. "At the far end. Come on. I'm hungry."

Pen went on talking as they threaded a course through the tables. Amy led the way.

"Charming city," he said. "No doubt about that. Good place to spend money when you've got any. Wedding cake Civic Centre and all that. But there's no power here, see. Anybody with a minimum of political sense can see that. It's what you call provincial. You know what I mean? Everything about it is essentially provincial. Cosy, no doubt. Nice and friendly in a vapid sort of way. But essentially provincial. The architecture. The newspapers. The shops. The culture. The people. Anaemic and provincial. Nice-nice and nothing-nothing. There's more real spark in one valley than the whole of this confection put together and multiplied by a hundred."

He sat at the small table well satisfied with his own eloquence. Amy was not so impressed.

"You sound just like Leo Galt," she said.

She glanced at the menu as something she had read often before.

"I'm going to have poached haddock," she said. "Will you have the same?"

As they waited for the food to arrive he smiled at her across the table.

"All theory, am I? Is that what you think? Bit of a miner escaped from the coal face and the daylight gone to his head?"

Amy gazed fondly at his startling blue eyes.

Like stars on a frost they were twinkling with an excitement she had to

96

wait to share. He pushed a finger between the collar of his shirt and his neck. The collar was high and tight. The red tie had a small knot. He leaned over the table to speak to her more confidentially.

"I'm going to Russia." he said.

The blood drained from Amy's face. He did not seem to notice the effect his words were having.

"When?"

She struggled to control herself.

"Soon."

from *The Best of Friends* (1978)

IDRIS DAVIES

A Day Out

We went to Cardiff when the skies were blue
And spent our shillings freely
In Queen Street and the bright arcades,
And in the cockle market.
And dainty little typists and daintier little gentlemen
Smiled most scornfully upon our cruder accents.
But we were happy unambitious men
Ready to laugh and drink and forget,
And to accept the rough and ready morrows
Of the mining valleys.
We tasted strawberries and cream,
And perhaps we thought our transient luck would last,
And perhaps we dreamed a little in Cathays,
And we crowded into cinemas and cafés,
Or danced at evening, or sought a burning wench
And told her many tales.

And in the night, we laughed our way back home again
In trains that whistled merrily.
And some would open carriage windows
And gaze upon the stars above the Severn plain.
And some would jest about a woman,
And some would slip into a perfect sleep.

Back in our homes, by flickering fires,
We bade the day farewell in careless language,
And sought the simple beds of happy men.

W.J. GRUFFYDD

I do not Live *Here*

The truth is that I have never lived in a community since I left Llanddeiniolen for Cardiff a quarter of a century ago. Here I simply reside — sleeping, working and eating. I do not *live* here. At home in the village where I was reared I was part of one large community. I knew all about Elin Owen next-door, and her husband, Gruffydd Owen the sailor; when I heard laughter through the window, I knew for certain who was there; when a child passed by on the road, I could tell the history of its father and mother and grandparents; I knew where its great-grandparents lay buried, to what chapel they went, and I could relate many of their sayings. When I was a child, I could describe the mantelpiece of almost every house in the whole neighbourhood; I knew the houses where there was a portrait of Garibaldi painted on glass, where a set of the *Gwyddoniadur* (Welsh Encyclopaedia) was to be found, who had a yellow cat called Sam, and where there was a glass rolling-pin up on the wall. I knew how all the neighbours would react in given circumstances, where I should be most likely to receive a favour and where it would be unwise of me to say too much about myself.

Things are very different indeed for me now. Most of my neighbours are English or Scots, and the native Glamorgan blood flows pretty thin by this time through the veins even of those who call themselves Welsh. No-one around me speaks my language or thinks the thoughts I think; they are all rootless people, and none of them will be buried with their fathers. In a way it is more comfortable to live thus: there is such a vast continent between me and my neighbours that they never interfere, and I dislike interference. But how sad it is that a Welshman should be an exile in Wales, for every Welshman living in Cardiff or its suburbs is an exile. When I first came here, the farmers around and even the petty squires were Welsh-speaking; by today they have all gone. This morning I noticed that the cart of the milkman who calls here had painted on it the name of his farm — mis-spelt 'Pant y*n* Asgallen' instead of Pant y*r* *Y*sgallen; but alas, neither he nor his family knows any better. The last of the old Welsh farmers, Mr George, of the Deri, died a few years ago, and by today most of his land is covered with all kinds of monstrosities of houses and bungalows, with names no less monstrous.

Sometimes, in my bed when I cannot sleep, I bring to mind the homes of my native place, and I repeat the name of everyone who lived in each of them in my time or in the time of my parents; and after dropping off to sleep, I dream of the old people who have gone: my father and mother, my grandfather and my grandmother, my aunt Elin Huws of Cae Meta, Dafydd and Lewis Huws; and for a moment on awaking, I feel overwhelming happiness because I can still have their company. I don't know what Freud and Jung would say about this, and I don't care.

translated by D. Myrddin Lloyd from *Hen Atgofion* (1936)

ALUN LLYWELYN-WILLIAMS

Remembering the Thirties

In those painful days, we knew
who the enemy was: the sleek, corpulent capitalist,
the lunatic politician, and the guilty scientist:
it was easy to recognize the authors of our cancer and our disease.

On the edge of the city, the furrows of the unfinished street
fell into the rubble of the night, and the lovers
disappeared there two by two, like anxious missionaries
into the barbarians' cauldron, into the ashes of the world.

In fear we awaited the apocalyptic judgement,
in fear — and in joy. For this were we born,
to confidence in the destruction of false idols; we were privileged
in our anger, and in our pity for the poor and lonely.

We did not see, at that time,
the Black Sow lurking in the fierce bonfire,
nor the devil craving for the pigs' souls.

translated by R. Gerallt Jones

DANNIE ABSE

Wandering Welsh Jews

We were wandering Welsh Jews. I was born in Whitchurch Road, Cardiff, but after a year or two we were on the move. To 289 Albany Road, Cardiff. A few years later the wanderlust possessed my parents again and we shifted three minutes away to 237 Albany Road. A few years of stability and doors slamming before we trekked another 500 yards to 66 Albany Road. Was this an advance? We were nearer to the Globe Cinema now, where for 4d on a Saturday morning I could watch Tom Mix or Rin Tin Tin from the classy balcony and gob down on the kids who'd paid only 2d in the stalls. But my parents remembered the good old days at 289 Albany Road so, soon, we made Pickfords happy and moved back threequarters of a mile in that direction to 66 Sandringham Road. "Sixty-six is our lucky number," my father said doubtfully.

Why did we move so frequently from rented house to house? Because the bathroom needed redecorating and had begun to look like a grudge; because, though the jokes remained the same, my father's fortunes changed; because the mice had taken to chewing aphrodisiacs; because of Dai or Ken or Cohen the Crooner — for truly, sometimes, it is easier to move house than to get rid of certain guests.

I liked Cardiff. Until I was eighteen all that I felt attracted to, all that I loved was circumscribed by its boundaries. Yet I must have had some curiosity about other cities, other countries, for I recall asking my mother, "Where does England begin?" She promptly pointed to a nearby convenient railway bridge that crossed over Newport Road: "By there," she said. Though she was twenty-five miles wrong I thought for years that this side of the bridge was Wales where dark-haired men were human-size, 5 feet 8 inches like I am now, whereas eastward — "over there" — the wrong side of that significant bridge, strode alien flaxen-haired Englishmen affected with pituitary trouble.

South of our district, too, lived dangerous giants of a sort. Why else was I not allowed to go beyond Splott to the docks? "People get knifed in Tiger Bay," my mother warned me. Frankly, it was none too safe north of Albany Road either, for Philip Griffiths lurked there ready to bash me simply because he was a year older than I was or because I preferred

Eldorado ice cream to Wall's, or because I considered J.C. Clay a better bowler than Verity. Worse, after dark, coming home that way I had to pass St Margaret's Church graveyard where ghosts, magnified amoebae, slipped their chains so that between lamp- posts I would have to run faster than my own long shadow.

No, west was best. The direction of a 2A tram to Victoria Park where Billy the Seal swam in pond water that needed a wash and where nearby, in a house called Mon Repos, lived Margaret Williams who wore no knickers.

West is best. I'd go that way 'into town' when mitching from school so that I could hide in the echoing acoustics of the National Museum where I would stare for hours at the illuminated tanks of tropical fish or at the glass-eyed stuffed animals caught forever in petrified movement. West was the direction of pleasure. Summer holidays and occasional Sundays my father would drive us to the nearby grey sullen sea of Penarth or Cold Knap or Ogmore-by-Sea or Porthcawl. Or back to where my mother was born — Ystalyfera — where she would converse in Welsh while the rest of us would listen without passports.

West was also the direction of religion. For I would have to travel that way to reach Windsor Place Synagogue and to that piece of holy ground near the secretive River Taff. That ground, where even tries were converted, was called Cardiff Arms Park, and there huge crowds would religiously sing 'Land of My Fathers', a national anthem that is half a dirge and half a battle cry.

I suppose most youngsters vacillate between fear and happiness. Midway is boredom. And boredom, too, is big on the map of Cardiff, for it is a rainy city where children press their noses against window glass and whine, "Mama, what shall I do now? What can I play now?" But when the sun is out, what a handsome city Cardiff is. When I return there now and loiter a bit — say at Roath Park Lake where I regularly swam as a boy until I got a duckshit rash — I am surprised how naturally beautiful are those places I once played in. I never realized this as a schoolboy. Few of us when young are enraptured by nature as Wordsworth was. (Don't your children sitting in the back seat of the car — when you cry, "Look! Look!" at a sunset or some dizzy vista — continue to quarrel or read their comics?) I certainly did not realize how charming are the corners of Cardiff.

But it's a long time ago now since, standing below Cardiff Castle, I was Robin Hood halfway up the tower — which I remember one guide saying

103

was built in the sixteenth century, oh aye, during Queen Victoria's reign. And it's a long time since I first stood on the terraces of Ninian Park when Cardiff City was bottom of Division 3 (South) and the brass band played 'Happy Days are Here Again' while I imagined myself to be their new signing about to change the soccer destiny of Wales.

Such triumphs would make 'them' put up a blue plaque for me like they did for Ivor Novello on that house he once occupied in Cowbridge Road. But they would have a problem. Which house would they choose? Would it be 289, 237 or 66 Albany Road? Or 66 Sandringham Road, or 66 Vaughan Avenue in Llandaff, or that house in Windermere Avenue half bombed during the Second World War (while I was in it) or 198 Cathedral Road? (Cathedral Road was once the 'Arley Street of Cardiff, mun).

Well, since I'm dreaming why shouldn't I go the whole hog? Let them put blue plaques on the lot. Yes, so many blue plaques with the words: 'Family Abse, wandering Welsh Jews, lived here.'

from *A Strong Dose of Myself* (1983)

IDRIS DAVIES

Tiger Bay

I watched the coloured seamen in the morning mist,
Slouching along the damp brown street,
Cursing and laughing in the dismal dawn.
The sea had grumbled through the night,
Small yellow lights had flickered far and near,
Huge chains clattered on the ice-cold quays,
And daylight had seemed a hundred years away . . .
But slowly the long cold night retreated
Behind the cranes and masts and funnels,
The sea-signals wailed beyond the harbour
And seabirds came suddenly out of the mist.
And six coloured seamen came slouching along
With the laughter of the Levant in their eyes
And contempt in their tapering hands.
Their coffee was waiting in some smoke-laden den,
With smooth yellow dice on the unswept table,
And behind the dirty green window
No lazy dream of Africa or Arabia or India,
Nor any dreary dockland morning,
Would mar one minute for them.

DANNIE ABSE

Keith and Lydia and Me

We walked towards the fields; it was dusk now and the skies had changed to translucent green and purple. We strolled through a gate, puffing cigarettes madly, Lydia between us. On an allotment, a man wearing bicycle clips looked up at us amused. Towards Cyncoed you could see the wooded hills. Below us, the lights of the City and the Bristol Channel. The grass lay wet with dew and in the farther field there was a ground mist. Behind us, the allotment man, now chopping wood, disturbed the loneliness of the fields.

"I think I'll turn back here," said Keith suddenly.

"Why?" asked Lydia. "It's quite early yet."

"No, I've to be home early," Keith said, inspired. "Dad's got sciatica — and he's not to worry about me . . .".

"Psychosomatic?" I said.

"Yes," said Keith sadly, "psychosomatic."

"What is?" asked Lydia.

"His sciatica," I explained.

"You know what psychosomatic means, surely?" said Keith.

"Of course she does," I said.

Lydia smiled . . . I didn't like it that Keith thought Lydia stupid. Keith threw his cigarette-end on the grass and stepped on it professionally.

"Do you have to go, Keith?" I said.

"But definitely."

"Shall we walk back with you?" asked Lydia.

"Heavens, no!" I protested. "Keith's not afraid of the dark, are you?"

"No," said Keith mournfully.

"I'm so sorry you have to leave us," I said.

"We could walk back with him," suggested Lydia.

"No . . . oh no . . . please . . . please . . . don't spoil . . . your walk . . . because of me . . .".

"Not at all, Keith," Lydia sympathized.

"Well . . . you'll probably get back quicker if you're on your own," I said.

"Yes . . . probably."

"What a shame your father has sciatica," said Lydia.

KEITH AND LYDIA AND ME

"Well, good-bye, Keith," I said finally.

"Good-bye," he frowned, shaking hands with Lydia. "Give my condolences to Nancy." And then to me, "If you can't be good, be careful." . . . I laughed awkwardly. We watched Keith strolling down the path, past the allotment. The man who had been chopping wood came out on to the path, pushing his bicycle, and Keith opened the gate for him. "Shouldn't we walk him back?" asked Lydia. "No," I said, "he likes walking home alone."

Keith turned round and waved. Then he shouted, "Shall I leave some fags with you?"

"Don't bother," I called back.

He waved again, sadly, and disappeared into the road, leaving Lydia and me high up in a spring-chilled field, close to a moon that hardly shone because it was not yet dark.

We continued through the fairy-tale fields up to our ankles in grey mist and I gave my school scarf to Lydia to keep away the cold. She looked lovely in my green and gold scarf. I hummed the school song to myself:

> Green and Gold, Green and Gold,
> Strong be our hearts and bold.
> To remain unsullied our Great Name
> Adding to Ancient Glory, Modern Fame.
> Green and Gold, Green and ...

I nearly stepped on some cow-dung, humming. At the top we gazed down at Cardiff, at the lights dotting the shadows below, window lights, lamp-posts, flashes of electricity from the trams. Away towards the direction of Newport a train rushed through the dark, a chain of lights, like a glimmering thought, across the blank mind of the countryside. Somewhere down there amongst the lights, Mother would be in the kitchen preparing the evening meal. Leo would be in his room writing a speech for some Labour Party meeting, rehearsing it perhaps before the mirror. Dad would be in the armchair under lamplight reading the *South Wales Echo*, the spectacles slipping down his nose, and his mouth silently forming the words as he read.

"I think Keith is very nice," Lydia said.

"Yes, he's a good chap," I condescended.

"And attractive too."

I looked at her — was she joking? "Do you think so?" I asked doubtfully. I tried to see Keith through the eyes of Lydia. A scruffy, scraggy youth with red-brown hair falling over a high forehead without fuss — the freckled wide flat face, the snub nose, and eyes blue as a poison bottle. . . .

"Oh, I don't mean physically," said Lydia.

"No?"

"But he attracts me mentally."

"That so?"

I was taken aback. Imagine *anybody* being attracted to Keith *mentally*. Perhaps Lydia was a little backward after all! But Lydia slipped her hand into mine.

"Of course *you* attract me mentally *and* physically," she reassured me.

"I don't know why," I said, "there's nothing to me." I looked at her beautiful face. "Nothing at all really."

"Oh, but there is," protested Lydia.

"Besides, I'm no good for women," I pointed out. "I'm so selfish, so egocentric, inconsiderate. And I'm moody, shockingly moody. I think of suicide quite a lot, you know. I'd be hopeless to live with. Can't do anything in the house. Only concerned about myself. Yes, I'm an evil influence on women."

"You shouldn't speak of yourself that way," said Lydia passionately. "You're a good person."

"Oh no," I protested, "I'm rotten really. I know myself. Rotten through and through."

The fields traced our signatures in moonlight and shadows. Under the clear stars we looked at each other with wonder, anew.

"You're beautiful in this light," I said.

Lydia looked down at her feet.

"I'm going to kiss you," I said.

She feebly tried to stop me. After she said: "You're not like other boys. You kiss differently. You don't make me feel sick when you kiss me." I wondered how other boys kissed her and *which* boys.

"How do you mean?" I questioned her.

"You keep your lips closed when you kiss," she whispered. What did she mean? Of course I kept my lips closed. Was there another way of kissing?

I tried to embrace her again but she pushed me away saying:

"A girl mustn't be cheap with her kisses."

We turned back down the path and later I stepped on the cow-dung which earlier I had avoided.

from *Ash on a Young Man's Sleeve* (1954)

DOUGLAS HOUSTON

First Impressions

Disjointed clarities compose
An infancy in Cardiff:
The last tram in its finery of flags
Is fixed on memory's retina as it clanks
Down Whitchurch Road past the end of our street.

There's no municipal date-stamp on the rest,
Though doing what so many others did,
Peddling a paddle boat and netting minnows
In Roath Park, or the summer train to Barry,
Locates such glimpses in a common history.

There was a circus where the knife-thrower impressed me,
Prelude to the blade's instant in my brother's nose,
Maternal retribution's storm, and then the plum
That Nana slipped me as I sobbed beneath the table.
The eddies in the stream of undistress are few,

But there are pools whose depths are first sensings of death:
The scarlet berries with their bitter-smelling juice
Called *poisonous* on a walk down Canada Road
Spelled out mortality's one-minus-one,
Helped me make sense of Cathays cemetery,

Those acres of stillness behind the battlement wall
Where stone angels made heaven a cold enigma.
A short walk from the house, I often went with Nana
To visit her husband and their first son,
Who, it was explained, were actually buried here,

Unlike the Grampy who still drove a trolley bus
And other uncles I was used to seeing.
A sequence of questions while she changed the flowers

110

Turned up the facts right down to worms and dust to dust,
Opened a vault of awe I still frequent.

Visits most years review memory's archive
On where and who I was till I was five,
Though change takes much where the last tram has gone,
With several who augment the cemetery's aura,
Where love's the only home the past can have.

DANNIE ABSE

The Game

Follow the crowds to where the turnstiles click.
The terraces fill. *Hoompa*, blares the brassy band.
Saturday afternoon has come to Ninian Park
and, beyond the goal posts, in the Canton Stand
between black spaces, a hundred matches spark.

Waiting, we recall records, legendary scores:
Fred Keenor, Hardy, in a royal blue shirt.
The very names, sad as the old songs, open doors
before our time where someone else was hurt.
Now, like an injured beast, the great crowd roars.

The coin is spun. Here all is simplified,
and we are partisan who cheer the Good,
hiss at passing Evil. Was Lucifer offside?
A wing falls down when cherubs howl for blood.
Demons have agents: the Referee is bribed.

The white ball smacked the crossbar. Satan rose
higher than the others in the smoked brown gloom
to sink on grass in a ballet dancer's pose.
Again, it seems, we hear a familiar tune
not quite identifiable. A distant whistle blows.

Memory of faded games, the discarded years;
talk of Aston Villa, Orient, and the Swans.
Half-time, the band played the same military airs
as when the Bluebirds once were champions.
Round touchlines the same cripples in their chairs.

Mephistopheles had his joke. The honest team
dribbles ineffectively, no one can be blamed.
Infernal backs tackle, inside forwards scheme,
and if they foul us need we be ashamed?
Heads up! Oh for a Ted Drake, a Dixie Dean.

'Saved' or else, discontents, we are transferred
long decades back, like Faust must pay that fee.
The Night is early. Great phantoms in us stir
as coloured jerseys hover, move diagonally
on the damp turf, and our eidetic visions blur.

God sign our souls! Because the obscure staff
of Hell rule this world, jugular fans guessed
the result halfway through the second half,
and those who know the score just seem depressed.
Small boys swarm the field for an autograph.

Silent the stadium. The crowds have all filed out.
Only the pigeons beneath the roofs remain.
The clean programmes are trampled underfoot,
and natural the dark, appropriate the rain,
whilst, under lamp-posts, threatening newsboys shout.

BOBI JONES

Cardiff

Here where the Taff ebbs its sort of one-man sea
Between the walls of a vein with no love of the black haemorrhage
There is a taste of despair, bridges of traffic to everywhere
Not reaching any, and all the wet past
Not belonging to the future. Here the Taff ebbs.

And I, as a lad open to spirits,
Language happened to me as a world occurs.
It dripped on me, took possession like a healthy ocean,
Formed waves around me and swelled an easy shoulder,
And yet fresh, pure, clear as water,
And drowned me.
There is something not recognized in water.
It is air that's heavier but without the distance of air
Be it on the edge of a lake like a white limb, in a mist of breath,
Or on the bank of a brook, its stars a fairground without sobriety,
Or the sea, the sea is a swan that moves
Across the sad bosom of our eyes without pining,
Moving with the power and the thickness of silence.

Water extends our meaning: it is the joiner,
The surround of our feeling, deep to the lip:
In baptism it is tranquil as a maiden's sleep
Touching our dry foreheads with knowledge of pain.
It comes into our hands like an animal;
It slips from our grasp like a life. But it is a spirit,
A spirit that's cold on legs. The earth's shirt.
The restless laughter of seashore nights.

When I was a lad in body, the Welsh language
That once splashed through the fun and majesty of courts,
But now sucks the meaning of our remnants together,
It was. How to word the beating of the heart?
The receiving on my forehead? It guided me

From hard streets, through corridors of clerks,
Foul their envy and their self-conceit of bricks,
Along pound notes and nice lusts
To a bay. Oh how to tell of the kick of my eyes
On seeing the difference between what I was
And the chance to be whole as I had not dreamed of being?

Yes, water that scurries down to the roots is blood,
Collecting, a pool by holes of sap. It freshens
Clay soil that has had only hot-beaked hardship.
It is round, red as an apple. And Oh it runs
Among rushes like a girl, like a squirrel between the banks.
You'd laugh if you saw how babyishly
It clings to pebbles, its nose and its feet
And its tiny hands groping. It throws
Arms around joy; the drops dance
On heads like locks of hair quicker than reeling rays.

With the leaden rain in the pure evening,
With the heavy water along this ground
The language falls word by word before the wrinkled wind,
Leaf-drops in the mist. Mist.
The standards have fallen, and now the words,
Red, yellow, brown, white, whirl towards the ground
To lie, how long, before they are rotten powder.

Here where the Taff ebbs its sort of one-man sea
The water retreats, swirling, sour sludge
And a stagnant pool. Will there be anything further anywhere here?
A raw dry plain? Crumpled leaves
Without blue depth? . . . If so, let us rejoice
For the water that is left here; and not hoard.
Cheers, good luck, to God who has been moving
On the face of the waters. Cheers to Him
Who would raise living waters from a nation's well.

translated by Joseph P. Clancy

115

HERBERT WILLIAMS

A Celebration

You will know it, the ragwort,
Though not perhaps by name —
A yellow flower, full
Of mischief for the gardener.
A common weed, populous
As common people, and as apt
To make the best of an indifferent lot.
You will know its pertinacious ways.
Its bland possession of a tumbled soil.
And you will wonder why
I celebrate its impudence.

Well, I will tell you. There is a spot
In Cardiff where the Taff
Flows between grubby banks. The view
Is nonexistent. Concrete, bricks,
And traffic brash as pain.
Between the road and river runs
A row of rusty railings. And just here
The ragwort grows. A common weed.
But such a blaze of beauty that it blooms
Redemption on the urban blasphemy,
And justifies itself like Magdalene.

EMYR HUMPHREYS

After the Match

Packed tight between the south stand and the car-park the crowd oozed good-humouredly towards the Westgate Street gates. Collectively it was digesting the game like a good meal. Wales had played with resolution and the necessary flashes of brilliance and they had won by two converted tries to a penalty goal. Eruptions of laughter and shouting from groups whose enthusiasm was still unspent caused some to turn their heads in the hope of extracting the last drops of pleasure from the expiring occasion. The wave of movement halted. There was a solid block of humanity at the gate, all facing east, several thousand necks protected by collars and scarves against the stiff breeze that had kept the rain off for the duration of the match. It was possible to squint upwards and wonder how much lower the clouds could sink before the rain fell; but impossible to pull a hand out of a coat pocket and bend an elbow to insert the stem of a pipe between the teeth. Friends who had not stuck close together from the moment they moved from their position in the stands or the enclosures would not see each other again, unless they had made prior arrangements to meet at precise rendezvous and at precise times. More than a couple of yards apart and the faint illusion of controlling your own destinies dissolved completely.

Individuals were no more than corpuscles, obedient in the stream that controlled and conditioned their immediate existence. The skin and clothing in which each was wrapped served to emphasise their unity: as if they had been made up in a factory into shapes that gave the maximum cohesion.

Professor Amos, Doctor Hudson and Gwilym Tist were wedged together contentedly enough but beyond talking. (In such a crowd, at such a juncture, it is often easier to talk to a stranger than a friend.) Amos was the tallest. He looked ahead shrewdly but in fact saw little more than a further expanse of heads sprouting densely in the width of road beyond the gates. The professor's curly grey hair fluttered freely in the breeze and seemed a badge of his hardy open-air outlook and pursuits. Tist was a young lawyer who appeared regularly on television. He was so well wrapped and pale he could have been in disguise for this public occasion. He was also a parliamentary candidate who hoped to speak for the claims of Wales in the ranks of the Labour Party and he made it his business to look calmly patient. Doctor Hudson was a frail middle-aged scholar, a reader in Comparative Religion. Professor Amos looked down on him with brotherly concern. He called Dr Hudson 'Huddy' and addressed him in the familiar but friendly manner he always felt compelled to adopt when on a visit to Cardiff.

All three were members of an advisory council which tended to meet in Cardiff on dates that coincided with important rugby football occasions. Usually it was Professor Amos who would call out under 'any other business' — *Mr Chairman, before you come to the date of our next meeting, may I point out that the French match takes place on Saturday the twenty-sixth! In the capital city!* and then there would be laughter and winking among the council members around the long table as they fingered the thin pages of their pocket diaries. At first Dr Hudson had been unaware of the significance of these jokes. He had gazed absently at his colleagues over the top of his reading glasses and then hurried away to catch his train. . . .

The crowd began to move again, inching its way nearer to the gate. Helmets of policemen appeared, bobbing up and down like upturned boats moored on a narrowly limited horizon. Suddenly, out on the street, the crowd broke. The Professor placed himself in front of Dr Hudson and they were swept along towards the Angel Hotel. When it was at last possible to stop, the professor stopped and turned around.

"Where's Tist? Where's Gwilym Tist?"

He sounded fussed and anxious. Dr Hudson looked down at the toes of his boots and smiled. Most of the things the professor said and did seemed to give him a mild form of amusement.

"Don't tell me we've lost him?"

Inexplicably Gwilym Tist was ahead of them. Out in the Cowbridge Road, in the centre of an oasis of unpopulated road surface, the well-wrapped figure beckoned them to join him.

"Academics!" he said. "Out of training both of you. Come on now while the going's good."

"Not the back bar of the Park for God's sake," Professor Amos said. "It's full of boys and girls in college scarves who look too young to be there."

"Couldn't we have a cup of tea somewhere?"

Dr Hudson's slow North Wales accent sounded even more tentative than usual.

"Come on Huddy! In the interest of science. You've got to carry out

118

your researches into the Ritual unto the bitter end. 'Bitter' end. That's good GT. Did you hear that? The 'bitter' end."

They hurried down the street, hopping on and off the pavement to avoid people, and keeping Gwilym Tist in sight. He turned to wave them on and then dived into a side street. When they caught up with him he was already in conversation with the manager of the steak-bar who had kept a corner for Mr Tist and party as promised.

"What it is to have influential friends," Professor Amos said.

He was rubbing his hands and sniffing the smell of meat cooking on a grill in the far corner of the long room.

"Soft lights and sweet music!"

Professor Amos nudged Dr Hudson.

"Make a note of this Huddy. Just the place to bring one of those birds of yours."

Dr Hudson winked at Gwilym Tist who smiled indulgently. Pints of bitter appeared on the table as if by magic.

"I can't drink one of these," Dr Hudson said.

"Good for your kidneys," Amos said.

He drank down more than half his tankard in deep grateful gulps.

"Now then. Now then Huddy boy, what about your impressions?"

"Impressions of what?"

"Oh for God's sake man. Here you are. Just been taken to your first rugby international. First *ever*. Now then. What have you got to say about it?"

"It was very interesting."

"*Interesting!* Interesting! I'll tell you something Huddy. You are a complete mystery to me. What about all that stuff you were regurgitating after lunch about the nature of crowds?"

"I've forgotten what it was I said...".

Again Hudson winked slyly at Gwilym Tist. The professor waved his hand as if he were feeding a reluctant student in a seminar.

"What kind of a crowd was it to begin with? Tribal? Religious? Power-directed? Destructive? Constructive?"

"I know one thing," Gwilym Tist said. "I wished I'd stayed at home and watched it on television."

"Gwilym!"

Professor Amos sounded horrified.

"You're getting soft man. A boy of your age. It's disgusting."

"Seriously. I hardly saw anything of the first half. And my knees were

119

cold. And I'm fed up with being washed in a sea of nostalgic song. You're quite right. I am soft. Sad, isn't it?"

"It was a good crowd."

Dr Hudson made the statement solemnly.

"Shush! The oracle is speaking. That's the trouble with these North Wales wizards. You have to wait so long before they pronounce. Look at this."

His knife was already in his hand as he pointed at the garnished steak which had been placed before him.

"They're laying this on for you, Gwil. All out to impress you, eh? The TV star!"

He nudged Dr Hudson.

"I hope you realise, Huddy, we're living in GT's reflected glory."

"I'm afraid we got them their licence. It was quite a battle."

Gwilym Tist looked around the interior and shook his head sadly.

"The owners don't have too good a reputation."

Professor Amos chewed hard at his steak.

"The bubble reputation...".

"I'm afraid you have very few illusions if you work in a law firm."

Dr Hudson was staring apprehensively at the size of the steak on his plate.

"There's far too much here for me you know. I eat very little meat."

"Scruples?"

The professor was chewing hard at his mouthful.

"Most over-rated dish in the world, I'd say," Gwilym Tist said. "It's just a great big tasteless cult for retarded adolescents. Really now, I mean it."

"Well, on behalf of the retarded adolescents may I say this is very good? Get some beer down you, boy," the professor said. "The world will look better then. Don't you know Wales has just scored a famous victory?"

Gwilym Tist lifted his glass in a silent toast. They ate and drank, enjoying their meal after two hours in the open air. Amos unbuttoned his waistcoat and spoke appreciatively of the comfort and the good food. It was the middle of the meal before he remembered to press Dr Hudson once again for his view of the match.

"It's an impressive sight," Dr Hudson said. "The green arena. The stands and terraces packed with eighty thousand people. The entire population of my county. And thirty young gladiators in peak of fitness, ready to do battle."

"Ready to set right Wales's ancient wrongs, eh? Ready to pulverise the oppressor. Ready for the sweet scent of victory."

Dr Hudson shook his head.

"No. It wasn't that. What impressed me was the longing in the stands for a vanished youth. That was one thing. Rows and rows of grey-haired men with red faces from drinking, smoking and overeating, reliving an idealised youth, identifying with the young heroes in the arena. To see that collectively, that was interesting. I would have thought that was the core of the cult really."

"Beating England, man. Or anybody. All comers ...".

"No."

Dr Hudson pushed shreds of meat out of his top teeth with the tip of his tongue.

"No. Not winning. Avoiding losing. Avoiding failure."

"What's the difference?"

"There is a difference. Not losing means avoiding failure. Avoiding the common fate. Analogous to postponing death. This is why the ritual is not really religious. And not so much sublimated warfare either. It's probably more sexual."

"Oh-oh, here we go."

Dr Hudson frowned as he chewed. He was thinking aloud.

"I suppose the sources of aggression are the same. I shall have to give it rather more thought. But you asked me for my impressions. It was interesting. Of course I didn't understand the finer points of the game. It's quite complicated really. But of course that would be part of the pattern. Make it difficult. The testing of the hero. A mythological category."

"Come down to our level, now," the professor said. "What did you like about it?"

"That thing you called the 'Garryowen'," Dr Hudson said.

He smiled and with an unstraightened finger prescribed an uncertain parabola in the air.

"The old 'Up and Under'," Professor Amos said.

He became consciously daring.

"Well that's sexual if you like."

He laughed noisily and Dr Hudson, with his eyebrows raised to acknowledge the unexpected validity of the point, nodded sagely.

"The hero is subjected to certain tests and trials. Like the labours of Hercules and so on."

"Now there was a hooker for you!"

The professor's face flushed convivially. Three helpings of fresh fruit salad and cream appeared before them. The professor smacked his lips and Dr Hudson looked pleased.

"I eat a lot of fruit," he said.

from 'The Hero' in *Natives* (1968)

DANNIE ABSE

Return to Cardiff

'Hometown'; well, most admit an affection for a city:
grey, tangled streets I cycled on to school, my first cigarette
in the back lane, and, fool, my first botched love affair.
First everything. Faded torments; self-indulgent pity.

The journey to Cardiff seemed less a return than a raid
on mislaid identities. Of course the whole locus smaller:
the mile-wide Taff now a stream, the castle not as in some black,
gothic dream, but a decent sprawl, a joker's toy facsade.

Unfocused voices in the wind, associations, clues,
odds and ends, fringes caught, as when, after the doctor quit,
a door opened and I glimpsed the white, enormous face
of my grandfather, suddenly aghast with certain news.

Unable to define anything I can hardly speak,
and still I love the place for what I wanted it to be
as much as for what it unashamedly is
now for me, a city of strangers, alien and bleak.

Unable to communicate I'm easily betrayed,
uneasily diverted by mere sense reflections
like those anchored waterscapes that wander, alter, in the Taff,
hour by hour, as light slants down a different shade.

Illusory, too, that lost dark playground after rain,
the noise of trams, gunshots in what they once called Tiger Bay.
Only real this smell of ripe, damp earth when the sun comes out,
a mixture of pungencies, half exquisite and half plain.

No sooner than I'd arrived the other Cardiff had gone,
smoke in the memory, these but tinned resemblances,
where the boy I was not and the man I am not
met, hesitated, left double footsteps, then walked on.

HARRI PRITCHARD JONES

The Vigil

Watching the toing and froing of the windscreen wiper on the busdriver's window had almost hypnotised Gwyn. He'd chosen the seat immediately behind the driver's cab in order to be on his own. The streets were full of little lights impairing the darkness, and the wiper and the streaming rain smeared them and cleared them alternately.

Just in time he realised he'd reached the castle. He rushed along the bus and jumped off onto the busy pavement. He stood a moment then walked back a little along Queen Street, and into the 'Taff Vale'. It wasn't half as full as he'd expected, considering there were only three more shopping days to Christmas. Today he should have been going home for the vacation; setting off to Pontypool; changing there and in Shrewsbury. At least he'd managed to avoid that much tedium.

"What d'ye want, love?"

"Half of Rhymney, please, dear."

"Coming up." There's some advantage to being a regular.

The average age here tonight seems much higher than usual. I don't take much notice of these people in their chairs along the walls, and by the fire-place, when I'm one of the noisy over-confident gang at the bar. Those two old ducks would find it hard to hear themselves speaking if my crowd were here now, bellowing their songs out and laughing loudly. Though, perhaps, the pair of them would feel happier with a wall of sound surrounding them. Tonight they've got to whisper over their drinks and their shopping, turning now and then to check that no one can hear their terrible secrets. They needn't worry: the television set has its usual captive audience, even though, according to the strange custom of some pubs, the sound isn't even turned on.

Gwyn realised that Jenny, the barmaid, was too busy re-stocking the shelves to be able to talk to him, and found himself a chair, beside a sickly looking old man who had at least reached the promised age. He wore an old suit of coarse tweed, with a long, tattered overcoat draped over his thin shoulders and dangling on the floor. Across his waistcoat and nervous hands lay a gold watch-chain. You could see where his hat had flattened his thinning hair onto his skull.

Gwyn took out his *Echo*, and started reading, but soon got bored with the tiresome trivia of local news and put it down on the table in front of him. From the corner of his eye he could see the old man dozing; his head swinging back and forth like a china Mandarin, revealing the two old ladies, gossiping and sipping, each time his head lurched back. On the other side of the room, opposite the fire-place, sat an old lady, almost of a pair with the old man, but in much better nick. She sat behind a glass and a bottle of Guinness. Gwyn was startled to see she was reading *The Sporting Life*. Her eyes were full of life, and the flesh of her face firm and healthy. She was a small woman, and Gwyn suspected she'd put rouge on her cheeks. Her overcoat was shapely, almost elegant, of fine material and unadorned except for a thin edging of fur around the collar which had worn pitifully. On her head she wore a black straw box hat, with a cluster of wax cherries on its front. All bought for some wedding years ago, perhaps. From the cracks on their uppers and the worn heels, her shoes were probably every day ones by now.

Before long a similar version of humanity came in to join her, in a thicker coat with a plastic mack over it. Her hat was of feathers, rather like an ill-fitting bathing cap, clinging to her head and revealing how big her ears were. The first woman rose to buy her friend a drink, without consulting her first, and returned with a glass of port. The two of them started talking gaily.

"Excuse me," said Gwyn's neighbour, "d'ye mind me having a look at your paper?"

"Not at all."

A northern voice thought Gwyn, before retiring into his own company again. Who was it said everyone starts talking to himself as soon as he's on his own? Well, I've been talking to myself a lot more these last few days; more than I've done for ages — since my early teens probably. Wandering about the back streets of Adamsdown and Bute, then crossing the centre of town through Canton to avoid friends. A bus out to the Wenallt in the morning and a wander about up there. But tonight I feel safer here, with nearly everybody I know well gone home for the vac.

I was never in trouble like this before, God help me. What'll I do? I can't tell the family. No, I daren't tell them. I'm not even willing to accept the truth of it myself. All those years trying to put some shape on my clay; parents, teachers, friends — and even Yours Truly; according to varied expectations and ambitions. And now, when the final form is beginning to emerge, and the wheel to slow down, before the clay sets, this had to happen. Bloody hell!

I've strayed from the path on previous occasions, betrayed each and every principle I've ever held, I know. But this is different. There's something so final about it. I'd have to accommodate myself to it, and everyone who has anything to do with me. And I don't have enough fibre in me to stand such a thing. But what the hell will I do? I'd rather disappear than face matters; away on one of those gigantic ships down the docks, perhaps . . . or just disappear completely.

Probably they'd prefer me just to disappear into thin air rather than bring disgrace on the family. There's only one thing to be done. . . .

"Thanks, young man. . . . Quiet tonight, isn't it?"

"Yes, it is. You're from the north by your accent."

"Quite right," his voice was weak and hoarse. "But I've been down here for years now. Where are you from?"

"Near Caernarfon, Tre'r Waun."

"Well, well." The old man turned to Welsh. "I'm from Cerrig-y-drudion. What are you doing down here, college?"

"That's right." Gwyn rose hurriedly. "Another pint?"

"Thanks very much."

Gwyn went to fetch them.

"Cheers, my boy, and thanks again . . . I'd give the world to be your age now, and have your opportunities. Really I would. I'd been away at sea five or six years when I was your age, sailing out of Liverpool; deep sea, and every continent; seen the world! I remember when . . .".

In spite of himself, Gwyn's mind became bored with the conversation as the old man went on and on narrating the story of his life, remembering his arrival in the capital, his marriage and the birth of his kids, and their flight over the nest, migrating to England and to Canada. Then he'd lost his wife soon after retiring. The final part, where he concentrated on his woes and worries as a poorly off widower, further depressed Gwyn's spirits. His only responses were the odd "No!," "You don't say," or "God help you!" as the old man sailed through his peroration. Gwyn remembered he hadn't told his landlady that he wasn't going home for the vacation. If he was still here tomorrow, he'd have to face her. He had to decide what he was going to do.

The two on the other side of the old man had already left, having wished the barmaid good night, and the place was almost empty except for the two of them and the two women opposite who were stirring as if to go, and calling for a little parcel each from Jenny to take home with them. When they were leaving, they turned back, their few bottles tucked under their arms, and looked at the two men.

"Compliments of the season to you both," and to the old man, almost in unison, "Hope we'll see you here tomorrow, Tom. All the best now, and to you love." Gwyn smiled back. They threw a final good night at Jenny. As the door swung back and forth after they'd gone, a cold draught slipped in, and Gwyn decided to leave.

"Time I went too, grandpa." The old man's face had sunk, and he was dribbling slowly from the corner of his mouth. The veins on his folded hands stood out, blue against the pale, membranous skin. There was a good drop of beer left undrunk in his glass.

"He's worse than usual tonight, poor chap," said Jenny. "Haven't seen him like this for a while . . . and the last time we had to get the police to take him home."

"No . . ." blurted Gwyn without thinking. "No, don't do that, whatever you do. . . . Where's he live? I'll get him home somehow."

"God bless you, love, that's what I say. Gwyn, isn't it? . . . It's down the docks, behind the big Windsor somewhere. He's got a room of sorts; looks after himself after a fashion; comes up here for a couple of pints before doing a shift as night-watchman in the new bit of the university up in the park. He's got a couple of days off this week, though. . . . No family, I don't think . . . poor bugger!"

She'd come round to help lift him to his unsteady feet and hook his arm around Gwyn's shoulders. He noticed her slipping a packet of twenty fags into the overcoat pocket. One end of the watch-chain fell out, and as Gwyn returned it to the waistcoat pocket, he realised there was no watch at either end.

Gwyn took his leave, Jenny holding the door for them and watching as they stumbled down the back lane, in the general direction of the docks. The old man wasn't very heavy; suprisingly light in fact, and he did try to use his feet every now and then, with a prolonged sigh as he did so. He awoke gradually as the cruelly cold air groped under his clothes, and from under the railway bridge on he managed to stagger along without leaning too much on Gwyn.

When they got to Mount Stuart Square he began to mutter and gesticulate with his free hand. Eventually Gwyn understood that he was trying to point back along the way they'd just come. The old man took a deep, laboured breath and whispered, "Number 172 . . . top floor. . . . Thanks, my boy." His chin fell back on to his chest.

Having found the house, Gwyn fought his way up a bare staircase, and found the doorkey in a waistcoat pocket. A black man emerged from a nearby room, at the previous turn of the stairs. A white girl clung to his waist, and they shut the door on the noise of a party. The man propped the amazed girl against the doorpost and came to help Gwyn. They laid the old man out on his bed, then the stranger left without a word, just a tender smile as he closed the door.

Gwyn sat by the window. There was hardly room to swing a cat. A raincoat and a tweed jacket hung on a peg behind the door, and in another corner there was a small paraffin stove with a kettle on it. On a small table, covered with an oilcloth, there were the remains of a loaf, half a pound of margarine in use, a knife and teaspoon. The light bulb, hanging from the centre of the ceiling, had a layer of grease and dust on it, and it hardly shed any light on the high, upper reaches of the room. Gwyn was appalled to see the filthy bedclothes as he went back to the old fellow, but did manage to remove his outer garments and shirt collar and, by rolling him gently from side to side, to get some bedclothes over him. Throughout the distressing process the old chap sighed intermittently, quietly, half-opening his eyes as he did so. Gwyn went back to the chair, and listened intently to the breathing until it settled into some sort of rhythm again, and then became quieter, as he seemed to sink right into the mattress. It became so quiet indeed that Gwyn went over to make sure he was still alive, and felt for the pulse at the wrist before feeling it was safe to leave.

He went over to the window first, to look down the street and noticed a Welsh Bible and Hymn Book on the sill, smothered in dust. As he descended the stairs he had to push his way through a small crowd leaving the party.

He welcomed the cold, fresh air onto his face, and turned to stare at the clock on the warehouse tower nearby. A quarter to one. He went down to the waterside by the quay where the ships sail for Somerset. The sea was quite calm and the night moonlit. Gwyn stared a long time at the reflection of the stars and the moon, as his own, unresolved problems flooded back into his mind. The sea looked warm and cosy. The sea never shows its scars; blows echo out in ripples which lose themselves.

A stronger breeze blew him off his thoughts, and shattered the reflection of the moon. Gwyn turned away, and walked briskly for a while until life returned to his numb limbs. There were still people moving about; the odd sailor staggering drunkenly back to his ship. The still of night doesn't last long down the docks. People at some business all the time, a motley crowd forged into a community by poverty and adversity. People who love to forget themselves in the fun-loving company of the sailors' pubs, with prostitutes full of gin and zest. It wouldn't be a problem down here. A man seems destined to hurt someone or other all the time, and it's a hell of a thing to have to take life-long responsibility for one mistake. He'd very nearly gone to the ultimate in self-interest tonight. The breeze was laden with seaspray, and his cheeks damp and cold. He shivered violently, but felt more awake then than he'd been for hours, and his mind clearer. It had turned one o'clock. There was nothing for it, was there, but to turn homewards.

translated by the author from 'Y Gwylnos' in *Storiau'r Dydd* (1968)

JOHN TRIPP

Capital

This will be the last ditch to fall
to the swing of its country.
Significance blowing down the hills
dies on the wind. Here the puffed
clink in their chains of office,
and the hagglers squat like a junta.

It is still as separate as an arm
lopped from its body: a strange sleeve
of territory spilled across the border.
What time has so carelessly mixed
clots here, where the ideals sag
and roots sprout only on the surface.

As long as I remember, the droll warmth
of its people has blurred
when our flag is lifted. Mouths are stitched.
Nothing is put to close scrutiny;
a knotted topic is flicked
into the bin, with a grin for Wales.

But now in the distance, I think I hear
the young villagers build our future,
laying the first bricks of change.
This capital means less to them
than the land, where everything stems.
"Wait," they are saying. "Wait for us."

ALUN RICHARDS

You'll not Move me an Inch!

Elmyra Mouth did not like *BBC Wales*. Either on the box or off it. Although she dutifully watched the programmes which involved her husband as assistant camera-man, she was always conscious of a great disparity between them and her. She did not like the announcers for a start. The women looked like something out of a Sunday School vestry and the men sounded phoney, half- London, half-Welsh, neither one thing nor the other, with the most unacceptable of getting-ahead acquisitions, posh accents.

Then again, on the few occasions when she went down from the valleys to Cardiff and waited for Davie in the staff canteen, Elmyra had increased her dislike for what went on behind the scenes. Take the bosses. They treated the more lowly technicians' wives like dirt, either looking through you, or rambling on amongst themselves in deep, book Welsh. Always jabber-jabber, it was, never mind whether you understood or not. They had no manners, Elmyra concluded, but that was not the worst. From what she had heard from Davie who was inclined to exaggerate to please her, the place was a hotbed of sex. You never knew who was sleeping with who, and for all the air of sanctity which somehow got on the air, behind the scenes, Elmyra was sure, the place was like a rabbit warren.

Wasn't it full of strangers? Glamorgan people lost out all the way along the line. You seldom came across anybody from the valleys, or Cardiff even, just the *in* Welshy-Welsh, catarrhal BA'd North Walians down for what they could get, Ministers' sons from everywhere, and girls from farms by the look of them, legs like bottles, all sitting around endlessly in the canteen, heads bent together and the hum of gossip rising like steam above a football crowd. Some of them *lived* in that canteen. It was an unhealthy atmosphere, Elmyra felt, and definitely not her style.

But there was another side to it. Her Davie had a good job by valley standards. On top of what he was getting in take-home pay, he always managed a few bob on top, what with car allowance, expenses and subsistence — it was as good as the Police from that point of view. But she had put her foot right down when there was any talk of moving down to Cardiff. Her grandmother had left her a furnished house, the corner one in the terrace, and where they lived, they had a view over the town that

131

was worth waking up for.

From the bedroom window, she could see right down Dan y Graig Street, over the rows of terraced houses below them, right down to the memorial park where the trees formed an avenue beside the confluence of the Rivers Rhondda and Taff. Further away, familiar grey mountains and brown tumps stood sentinel over other valleys, and everywhere she looked, Elmyra felt at home. Here she had a position and status, and although they used to call her Elmyra Mouth because of her not being backward in coming forwards in that direction, she was well content to be at home. She was a valley girl, was she not? She knew every brick of Dan y Graig Street, every shadow of the courting gullies behind the terrace, every blade of grass and *cwtch* on the bare mountain and tip behind, and although now you didn't hear the tramp of miners' boots in the mornings and the little front parlour shop around the corner no longer sold lumps of chalk for the colliers to mark their drams as they did in her mother's day, it was still home and here she felt comfy. So when Davie'd proposed moving to Cardiff as it would cut down his travelling time, she had a cryptic and typical answer.

"Travel you bugger," she said flatly. "You'll not move me an inch!"

from 'The Scandalous Thoughts of Elmyra Mouth' in *Dai Country* (1973)

GILLIAN CLARKE

Suicide on Pentwyn Bridge

I didn't know him,
the man who jumped from the bridge.
But I saw the parabola
of long-drawn-out falling in the brown

eyes of his wife week after week
at the supermarket cash-out.
We would quietly ask "How is he?"
hear of the hospital's white

care, the corridors between her
and the broken man in the bed,
and the doctors who had no words,
no common supermarket women's talk.

Only after the funeral
I knew how he'd risen, wild
from his chair and told her
he was going out to die.

Very slowly from the first leap
he fell through winter, through the cold
of Christmas, wifely silences,
the blue scare of ambulance,

from his grave on the motorway
to the hospital, two bridges down.
A season later in a slow cortège
he has reached the ground.

ROBERT MINHINNICK

Images from Tremorfa

The incense of a tall brazier
Like bitter odour of burnt horn
A hot acridity inside my head.

I slide off early over cushioned mud,
Passing East Moors, a blitzed town
Burning and deserted, fire's

Intricate horizon a yellow
Thread woven into the dark.
Moving alone on the grey sea-moor

After today's clerking of the ferrous trade
I remember the Greek in the precious-
Metal shop; Mr Stassinopolos,

His sweat a helmet of new steel
Tight across his brow, and the Furies'
Camp, caravans beneath the iron scree,

Dogs loping behind child acrobats.
Cold, cold with a vengeance now,
The winter light solidified, opaque.

For the last time I move through Queen's Wharves
And watch the derelicts, the fuse
Burning in their eyes; like terrorists

Carefully carrying the gelignite
Of their experience towards the town's bright glass.
Tonight, I share their cause, its sure defeat.

GILLIAN CLARKE

East Moors

At the end of a bitter April
the cherries flower at last in Penylan.
We notice the white trees and the flash
of sea with two blue islands beyond
the city, where the steelworks used to smoke.

I live in the house I was born in,
am accustomed to the sudden glow
of flame in the night sky, the dark sound
of something heavy dropped, miles off,
the smell of sulphur almost natural.

In Roath and Rumney now, washing strung
down the narrow gardens will stay clean.
Lethargy settles in front rooms and wives
have lined up little jobs for men to do.
At East Moors they closed the steelworks down.

A few men stay to see it through. Theirs
the bitterest time as rolling mills
make rubble. Demolition gangs
erase skylines whose hieroglyphs
recorded all our stories.

I am reminded of that Sunday
years ago when we brought the children
to watch two water cooling towers
blown up, recall the appalling void
in the sunlight, like a death.

On this first day of May an icy
rain is blowing through this town,
quieter, cleaner, poorer from today.
The cherries are in flower in Penylan.
Already over East Moors the sky whitens, blind.

GORONWY JONES

Daughters of the Dawn

The handy thing about Cardiff is you can get more booze after the pubs close with no trouble at all. In Caernarfon when I left you had a choice — the Cash Club or the Chinks. Now they've closed Cash and there's a fight in the Chinks every other Saturday night. That's one reason why a young chap like me who wants a bit of life is well-off here — for a while anyway.

Usually the lads from the Ely go to one of two places — the Casino in the docks or Papajios in the city centre. The Casino is hellish dark, dirty and noisy, and you have to get a taxi to go down there. If I had a rise I'd buy a small car. But there's beer in the Casino at prices that are not too bad. Wine, halves and shorts is what you get in Papajios, as I saw the other night.

"Pint of lager, please," I said the first time I went there. There's never mild in any club, I've found. It doesn't cost enough, and they want to skin you, aye?

"Only do halves. Lager's off. Wine or shorts?" this bird said curtly. What does it matter they're pretty if they talk so ugly?

"Bottle of wine then," said I. Cheaper than by the glass.

"What kind?"

"Any kind," said I, not understanding anything about them.

"Red?"

"Aye."

"£2 please."

"I only want one, aye," I said, but the bloody stuff was two quid a bottle! Do you through your nose. They're not more than a pound in the Howells' off-licence.

Peer through the dark and the cigarette smoke to see if I knew anyone. I saw Sabrina from *Pobol y Cwm* dancing with someone. I wouldn't have minded an autograph to show them back home I'm meeting the big nobs on the Cardiff scene, but I was scared of approaching her. I saw Wayne Harris there too but that's not who he really is because he also sings with Edward H. Davies.

None of the Ely lads, the shits, were willing to come with me because this was Thursday night.

"Come on, Stan," I said. "You all but live in that place and you've

136

boasted about it enough."

"Saturday night you'll get a wench there," said Stan. A wench is a piece and a spooner is a fellow. They're not all there down here in the South.

"Well," said I, "I've been carrying a pile of bloody big heavy Axminsters from the stores to the showroom all day and I deserve a drop." By the time I reached the Papa I'd decided to phone Mr Huxley the boss in the morning to say I was shaky — my back again. So down with the booze. . . .

"Martha Morris!"

"Do I know you?"

"Jesus. This one's got a memory like a sieve, aye?"

"Gron bach, I didn't recognise you with that red moustache."

"You like it? Trendy, aye?"

Martha was in the same class as me in Moriah Sunday school. She was in the grammar school and I was a bit lower down, aye?

"Where d'you hang out, Gron? Your mother was telling Dad in the shop that you were down here."

"I live in Roath, don't I, and I go to the New Ely just about every night. Never see you there, though."

"D'you like it there? Bit of a dump, isn't it?" she said, turning up her nose. There I was looking at her in her long flowery dress, her hair just-so and a lot of make-up and black eye-shadow and thinking she wouldn't fit into the Ely either.

"Sunday School and Band of Hope turned you against the booze, aye?" I said, pretending.

"Oh no. We go for a bit of a drink one or two evenings every week. Don't mention it to Dad, though. Conway, you know. Been there?"

"Yes," I said, but I didn't let on what a hell of a boring night I'd had there.

Then Luned and Gwenan and Siân joined us. Teachers every one living with Martha in Llandaff. I didn't fancy any one of them but they were standing in front of me like the Daughters of the Dawn.

"Gron comes from Caernarfon," Martha told them.

"Oh yes, where do you teach?" said Luned.

"I'm not a teacher." Why do they all think I'm a teacher?

"Oh!" said Gwenan. "Where do you join in Welsh life?"

"Don't worry, love. I've found the lads," I said.

"He plays cards in the pub every night," said Martha, and they all laughed and tut-tutted.

"And what do you do in the evenings, then?" I asked, a bit embarrassed.

"Well," said Gwenan, just about dying for someone to ask her, I think. "We're in the choir. The Urdd Choir and the Godre'r Garth Choir, about two or three nights a week. D'you sing? No?"

"Jesus Christ!" I said to the D.J. "Turn the bloody noise down, aye." "Hey, what does this guy want? Victor Sylvester?" he said.

Everybody was laughing at me and Gwenan went on: "And two of us have a night-class for Welsh learners. And we do a lot with the Urdd, don't we, girls? And Siân is Secretary of the local branch of the Blaid, aren't you Siân?"

Siân said nothing but smiled shyly and squeezed her handbag nervously. There was no need for her to be nervous, 'cause what about me having to listen to a gang of clever birds like this telling me how they were keeping Welsh alive in Cardiff? Made me feel hellish queasy, that I had no talent for anything, apart from playing not a bad game of darts or quite a good round of snooker, aye, and what use is that?

"Christ, girls," says I, "I thought I had done quite well to find a gang of Welsh lads to have fun with in Cardiff as if I was home in Caernarfon. I'm not good enough for your places, anyway."

"Come on now, Gronw," said ginger-headed Luned. Gronw? Why the hell is she calling me that? "The Urdd is open to everyone!"

The Urdd, like hell! I never belonged to the Urdd. I didn't want to say a word, either, because I knew Martha Morris had been a member from when she was so high. But she lived in St David's Road with the toffs, and that's who the Urdd lads were in Caernarfon. The children of deacons and teachers and the like. Folk-dancing and daft things like that. Cissies. Can you see the Sgubs lads going through a rigmarole like that? I remember Miss Jones Welsh giving out some Welsh comics to the class: "Only for the Urdd children," she said, and John Tŷ Nain and me pulling faces at each other. And I remember a bus full of them leaving the Maes in town for camp in Llangadog and singing stupid songs as they left. Down by the riverside, aye? John Tŷ Nain and I chucked stones at the bus as it started but I didn't want to upset these birds and so I kept my mouth shut.

I asked Martha what she was doing on Saturday night, but she was going to a wine-and-cheese party in Rhiwbina. And next week? Very busy, something on every night.

"How can you spare an hour to come here?" I said to her spitefully.

"Thursday night is a good night here," she said without taking any notice of me.

"A good crowd from the BBC comes here."

And I knew then it was here Martha Morris was looking for a chance to get off with someone and not among the town lads. There wasn't much shape to this shy girl Siân but I went across to her. I put my arm round her waist and I wasn't doing bad at all when, damn it all, a draught of the red piss I'd been drinking went down the wrong way. I choked on it and it spilled onto the mat, half through my mouth and half through my nose. The girls scarpered for fear of their long dresses catching it. Just as well, but not one bitch came to my assistance either when a sod of a bloody big bouncer came up and took me by the scruff of my neck.

"Out!"

"Not hellish likely, mate," I said. "I've just arrived after paying ten bob to come in, and paying two quid for this hellish bitter rubbish...".

But he was determined, and because I was determined too, things went haywire, didn't they? Before you could say Jack Robinson I was out on my backside on the pavement with this big sod kicking me all over. I was bruised all black and blue.

While I was still groaning on the floor two fellows came out of Papajios. The Manager and Gareth Connolly from the Ely. I didn't know he'd been there. They were quarrelling like the devil.

". . . and call your bloody animal off. I'm in the C.I.D. and I could get this place shut down tomorrow if I wanted to."

The manager turned all nice and helped me up and went through the motions of brushing the dust off my coat. Round the corner there was this club, The Revolution, where some pig of a bouncer killed one of the Cardiff lads about a month ago. There's a new name to the place now — Smileys.

Connolly and I walked home through the city sharing the bottle of wine he had brought out with him.

translated by Meic Stephens from *Dyddiadur Dyn Dwad* (1978)

139

DUNCAN BUSH

Back to Cardiff

The homecoming was always the same, the landscape
growing meaner mile by mile, the yards
of the intervening
farms as sordid as a gipsy settlement,

moored in the roads
of trampled mud
and rusting motor spares, ditched cars.

There is no greenness, only
the yellow fallow of dead grass,
nomadic sheep lost in a huge, bare field,
the white gulls scavenging inland.

Decrepitude and rust follow
the railway like a shanty town, like rubbish
strewing a trail into the city.

Scott sailed from this city
when it was young,
to die in the white Antarctic,
underneath the world.

The California Gold Rush
was undertaken out of both hope and despair.

The river lifts and drops
at the mouth of the salt tide. Above banks
of the alluvial, olive mud

the ponies are bowed
all day to crop subsistence, broken
by boredom, lashed
by slant grey rain.

The landscape
crowds with hedges, council houses,
recreation grounds. I was young here,
in the truant, errant holiday of youth.

The train slides
through the backs of the city.

It was later I yearned, heartsick,
for green, academic Summers.
So things drift, to knot.

Where is the may, the white
may, and the Midsummer's silver dream, lost
in the suburbs
and confronted with the Spring?

PETER FINCH

Painters

Me and Chico were sitting on the kerb sneezing. He reckoned it was hay fever but I thought that a little unlikely considering it was November. The wind still came in from the sea so we weren't that cold, just a bit wet. Chico talked a lot about snow, an obsession of his from childhood. He used to go out into it with a bucket and spade like it was sand. He'd stay there until his hands went so raw and red that he couldn't feel them. It wasn't my subject at all.

We were outside the city centre's last coffee bar in Charles Street. A scraggy building, painted about a bit with awful coloured emulsion and all scratched and scrawled with people's names. Coffee bars had died out as a profitable idea. All the kids would do was steal the sugar and carve slogans into the tables. Coffee was uneconomic. You could sit over it for three hours, sopping up someone else's heat and light. It was cheaper than being at home. Most of them closed, or went over to fast food. This last one was a sort of social thing run on city hall grants and urban aid. Lots of councillors and other worthies had had their pictures taken standing outside it.

Chico didn't want to go inside because he said it was like being tamed. "Once you go in there," his voice had a perverse huskiness to it for someone of five foot two, "they've got you. A youth in a youth club. Makes me think of churches and soap." He spat but it was half-hearted. Caught on his lip and ran a bit. Normally he could hit cars passing on the other side of the street.

I was all for going up Roath Park Rec., seeing if anything was doing, any decent women, a soccer match, something to shout at. Bloody boring where we were. But Chico was too tired.

"Do you think its getting colder?"

He blew into his hands. I sneezed.

"You want to get off your arse and run about a bit if it worries you that much."

Just then Billy Donald came round the corner on a nicked Tesco trolley. He was using it like a scooter. Over rough ground it wasn't that stable and he kept falling off. There was a lot of swearing and rolling on the floor. His coat had got all mangy and a few people had begun turning round to look at him. He gave them a quick flash, opening up his coat so they could see where he had sewn all manner of patches into the crotch of his jeans. Sign of virility he reckoned. Nobody looked of course — much too embarrassed — thought he might be displaying the real thing.

"How you, alright?" he yelled at me and Chico. "Keeping guard on the bomb for me then."

This was one of Billy's jokes, at least it had been a long time ago. He'd repeated it so often that it no longer even raised a smile. He meant, actually, the roughly boarded bit of demolition next to the coffee bar. The building that had once stood there had been knocked down under a corporation development only they'd run out of money or changed their minds and nothing'd been put in its place. The whole crumbling area was like that.

"You Nazis ought to be locked up you did," said Chico. He'd picked up the insult from slogans he'd heard bandied by the trendy left of the previous year. For a little bloke he had a nerve. The remark was missed by Billy or misunderstood, he carried on strutting about the pavement like Mick Jagger in the instrumental bits.

Actually Billy liked the idea of war and its macho excitement. He couldn't wait for the next one to start.

"Life's so damn straight it'd give us something to do. Bit of fighting. I'd be a pilot I would." He waved his hand around and made a roaring noise that was supposed to sound like a jet. "Smash 'em up with missiles and bombs."

"You're off your head Billy. They only need one bomb you know."

"Nah. They won't do that. Too quick. They'll have us all going round the place in tanks and boping each other. Get all the factories going again making shells. My old man told me that."

He leapt in the air and did a kind of kungfu chop with his feet at a rubbish bin fixed to the lamppost. It burst, sending paper all over the road. Billy didn't express any pleasure. He never did. I don't think he really noticed what he'd done.

"Bloody sissies," he shouted, "load of women, that's all they are."

Billy was a thorough conservative when it came to peace. Chico had lost the thread and wanted to leave Billy to all his arm waving and warmongering but I was sure if we walked off he'd only follow us. He was a natural trailer, never had anything better to do.

At this point, anyway, Billington showed up. Came out of the coffee bar like he was part of it, like it was the most natural thing in the world.

Bloody social workers all act the same. This one looked just like Ken Barlow without the stomach weight. Lank hair, *Guardian* in his pocket, plastic briefcase not even wide enough to carry a boiled egg stuffed all casual-like up under his arm. Billington wasn't a regular social worker. Didn't deal in nutters or old boozers or overly pregnant girls or anything like that. Projects was his field. Urban renewal. Load of whitewash really.

He waved at Chico, nodded at me, smiled at Billy like he was one of us, known us all our lives.

"You guys want something to do with yourselves." He said with fraternal concern, "Something to keep you on the straight and narrow."

His manner was a combination of middle-class fervour mixed with old-fashioned crap. Straight and narrow! What did he think this was, school?

Up until recently he'd had a curly beard all sprouting round his shirt collar. It made him look like a folksinger. Someone had told him this and he'd gone out and shaved it off.

"Okay Billington, man." said Billy, slipping into the vernacular, "where's it at?"

The social worker waved at the hoardings — cracked boards, defaced and stuck with fly posters — which surrounded the vacant ground.

"This lot's an eyesore, an awful untidy mess," he said. "I've got some council cash for paint. Tart it up a bit. Know anyone who'd be interested in doing the work?"

Chico studied the gutter, he wasn't the sort to get involved. I'd have put Billy down as the same only this time he surprised me. He stopped strutting and went right up to Billington and stared him in the face.

"How much?" he asked. You could tell he was interested by the way he was standing on his toes.

"How much! You've got to be kidding. You don't get paid for this kind of thing. You do it for the good of the environment. Score a few points for yourself. People won't be so hard on you then."

Billington was quite cunning. Billy was better.

"We'll do it," he said, "definitely."

He didn't bother to consult with Chico and me.

In the Golden Cross we had three halves. Couldn't afford more. Billy'd borrowed somebody's pint from the crush at the bar in order to top us up.

"They won't notice," he said.

I wasn't so sure. Then he explained what it was all about. We get Billington to pay us for materials. Keep the cash, nick the paint. Simple.

He showed us the inside pocket of his voluminous coat. It bulged with a

144

half litre can of gloss.

"Just get around the place asking for colour charts. No one will be suspicious. They don't expect anyone to go to the trouble of actually lifting paint."

When we were finally set up and actually got down to the job Billy turned out to have a real talent for what was in hand. He was skilled well beyond what anyone would expect from looking at him. He knew all about brush strokes, how to get a smooth finish, how to keep the colour inside the lines. Whereas me and Chico had paint in drips and splashes all over the shop, Billy's bits were perfection themselves. Before we'd started he'd drawn this huge outline and we were then supposed to colour the various parts in. Chico didn't like that. He liked writing. He wrote CHICO SCREWS WOMEN, foot high letters, in a tottering arc.

"Christ Chico," said Billy, "you're so bloody obvious. Can't you be more subtle about your predilections?"

Chico didn't understand this last word and somewhat overawed by Billy's skills decided that it would be better to paint it all out and start again.

When it was finished you could tell which sections Billy had done a mile off. His were clear, neat, sort of made sense. It was supposed to be the aftermath of war, a great scrapyard of jumbled shapes, bits of planes and tanks and guns.

"Appropriate ain't it?" He looked around for agreement, "this place being bombed."

We nodded, trying to get smears of non-drip gloss off our hands with damp rag and an old sliver of soap.

It wasn't all that easy in the pub afterwards. To start with Billy got accused at the bar of nicking someone's pint — which he hadn't done this time — and although normally righteously indignant was too tired really to put up much of a fight. Then when we'd got a few down us Chico was all for abandoning our Doc Martens in favour of smocks and sandals. He'd seen this in the cinema. "Artists get pissed like this all the bloody time," he kept saying. Chico was easily led. Anyway, someone complained about our swearing, well Chico's swearing I suppose, he was the one doing all the shouting, and Billy, all paint splattered, got into an argument with some well-dressed yob as to how he didn't ought to be in there, all filthy, messing up the seats for other people. Billy was going to put one on him, especially since he hadn't actually sat down yet, but recognised, I think, that things were collectively getting out of hand.

145

It was clear we'd have to leave when the landlord, a species not normally known for his tolerance but then no doubt he was thinking of his trade, started going on about fascists and racialists. Billy told him straight, we don't support the screwing Front, we're not all the bloody same. He banged the bar, knocked the ice bucket and spilled some old sod's half of dark. We had to leave.

When we passed the hoarding again the whole thing was harder to see. It was dark and on top of that we were full of drink. Billy was all arms and spitting, an aggressive caricature of his earlier self.

"See that," he bawled to no one in particular, "that's the tail plane of a B-52. They used them in Vietnam."

He whacked the wing mirror of a parked car to add emphasis to his statement. You could see a dark shape up on the depicted scrapheap that could just be what he said.

When we got closer we could see that a few additions had been made, a little political tidying to our exemplary work. TAKE THE TOYS FROM THE BOYS it read in huge white letters, WOMEN FOR PEACE AND AN END TO THE BOMB.

Billy stood there for a while staring at it. I thought for a moment that he was too drunk to read. Then he picked up a stone and threw it, splintering the wood, rushed up to the hoarding and started tugging at it, trying to pull it down.

"Bloody vandals," he shouted, as a half-wet section of painted ply cracked out of its framework. He whirled the piece furiously round his head.

"I'll give 'em cruise missiles if I get a chance."

There was a bit of consternation later when Billington found out what had been done. He wouldn't speak to us, just consulted, prodigiously, with his department on the phone. In the end it was agreed that public money was not for propaganda, no matter how clever. The whole lot had to come down.

Me and Chico waste our time now in the middle of it. They've turned it into a kind of park. Shrubs and raised borders, lots of tubs and benches, things like that. Billy's got a job. Joined the RAF at St Athan as an apprentice, paints the decals on the wings of planes. Funny really with him not being about but then a guy with a creative bent had got to be allowed to get on.

GERAINT JARMAN

January Song

Welcome
  to the new year!
  I wonder,
      where did the old one go?
A snow-shower came and overwhelmed it.

  Anything is possible.
  The fact that I am still alive
  bears this out.

  A door opens in front of me —
  I prefer new mistakes
  to the taste of certainty in my mouth,
  the taste of years gone by.

  Something new is beginning
    like a cry from the twilight,
  something new,
      the springs of the imagination
      and the heart;
here
in an old street,
that's where I live,
Alfred St
an english street
in an english city;
Cardiff,
the capital of Wales,
that's where I live,
live in a vacuum
searching for love.

  The seasons are difficult in a city,
    especially the seasons of the heart

because the heart's temperature
    changes,
every minute, every day, every month . . .
and the streets go on
    and go on
        and there's no getting away from them
and every street is part of the main road
    and the main road leads to
    another city
        and another . . .
and there's no getting away from them.

And what with all this
the year opens
    in the light darkness,
a new year to love, to deceive,
to hate, to get drunk, to decide,
to be happy, to repair, to count
tears, to tell a lie, to talk nonsense,
to create and to pull down . . .

feelings we didn't know about
    the greatness of little things . . .

    and what with all this
        the poem
            bursts into bud.

translated by Meic Stephens

SIÔN EIRIAN

My Square Mile

Once again the rain has come to sadden the city's streets. Cardiff rain is different from the rain that falls in Flintshire. It doesn't whip against the windows, nor does it whirl drunkenly in the wind's eddies, nor pummel old men's backs and blind old ladies' spectacles. Neither does it fall through the sun's sieve in small, warm drops to tickle the faces of lovers and moisten the noses of little dogs. No, Cardiff rain drips brownly from the sky, staining buildings and pavements with its filth.

But I enjoy walking the streets of the city when the shower is over. Interesting patterns along the paving, old bits of wet newspaper sticking to the heels of my shoes, and the gutters full of the rain's detritus: leaves and fag-packets and sometimes an old sock or a child's shoe. Piles of miserable rubbish. It's things like that give Cardiff its character. . . .

In two minds. Should I go across to the Park Hotel to beat up Stanley Morgan? The temptation is a strong one. I know full well that he goes there for a glass every lunch-time.

Last night, as I was walking along Clifton Street to buy pie and chips, I passed a shop-window renting television sets. And there on two or three screens in the window was the old, ugly clonk of Stanley Morgan. Jabbering and smiling through the folds of his fat jowls. I stood there watching him. He was on *Heddiw*, being interviewed at length about something or other. What, I wondered? The law? Cardiff's young offenders? The city's social problems?

What the hell does he and his kind know about Cardiff society and the background of the offenders he prosecutes or defends? The old collar-and-tie boar with oil on his hair and Old Spice under his armpits. Was he ever walking down Splott Road or Sanquahar Street around midnight to see his 'offenders' in their own setting? To see them rolling drunk out of the pubs and walking through the acres of rubble and the filthy streets, home to their impoverished families? Has he had to go to the Oxfam shop to buy clothes for his children? Has he got rats in his back-garden? Damp on the walls of his rooms and wooden boards instead of glass panes in his kitchen windows?

I'll have to beat him up, on behalf of the uneducated, uncultured, unprotected people of Splott. On behalf of the dirty little kids whose

149

fathers are in prison because of him. On behalf of the stupid parents with sons in Borstal as a result of his sweeping rhetoric in the magistrates' courts. And on my own behalf. I'll never forgive him for making me look a fool in front of the justices. For making my name appear in the *Echo*, ' "Anti-social" Cardiff man fined £56.' For making me lose three weeks' dole to pay the fine. Oh, there'll be revenge, oh yes, one day.

But not today. It's past three already. He won't be tippling in the Park now — he'll be back in court lambasting the character of some illiterate alcoholic of an Irishman and earning big money for doing so.

No, not today, but soon. . . .

Coming out of the Prince of Wales, and the city greets me with unexpected stillness. St Mary Street grey and empty; one car disappearing round the corner towards Penarth Road. Sunday evening, and this street, as busy as an ants' nest during the week, dead as a doornail tonight.

Standing there listening to the emptiness, a feeling of loneliness climbing through my body and pressing against my wind-pipe. A sort of sudden urge to hear voices and see colours alive and around my head. Wanting to convince myself that I'm among people, part of the city's living things rather than a motionless figure on an empty pavement at night.

Direct my steps towards the Duke of Wellington; walk short and fast through the filth and rubbish of Caroline Street — a street stinking of navvies' sweat, and the smell of chips, and graffiti and blood staining its walls.

Just about to step inside the bar of the Duke of Wellington, I hear the sound of Welsh singing sailing out of the chapel next door to the pub.

Pause, listen to the last verse of the hymn being sung and the sound swelling into a powerful crescendo towards the close. A familiar tune, although the words are beyond my recall. I must have sung that very hymn dozens of times when I was a child in the little chapel at Buckley. So nice to hear a Welsh hymn warming the night breeze in this old whore of a city.

And I'm still standing by the chapel railings as the congregation starts coming out in dribs and drabs. The twittering of their small talk filling my ears. The colourful splash of their hats and warm coats filling my eyes. Without understanding why, I begin walking leisurely along the pavement, past the front of the chapel in the direction of Hayes Island. I could have turned back, taken four steps into the lounge of the Duke of

Wellington. Because although these are all Welsh-speakers they have no idea who I am. I don't have to be afraid of them.

But, for some reason, I pretend to ignore the pub, and walk on as if I were on my way home from somewhere. And the congregation reaching the street, walking at my side and behind me along the pavement. For the first time since coming to this city, I'm lost in a sea of Welsh-speaking Welsh people! Hey ho! Wading in the sound of their talk and trying to catch every word.

"Yes, yes, very good."

"Goodnight now, Mrs Lewis. All right, goodbye."

"Where's your car?"

"There's ours. Oh, where's Eluned gone to now, I just . . .".

"The husband's car tonight, is it?"

"Is Mr Davies keeping well?"

"Yes, yes. Yes, next week."

"Brand-new. Seventy-eight pounds."

"We've got an automatic now, as well!"

"Oh, she was lovely, yes."

"And doesn't blue suit her so well!"

"Take care then, now. Good night."

And a woman or two still humming the old favourite hymns as they walk by. A young girl in her teens, in a long suede coat and white school socks, smiling sweetly and waving to someone in a car on the other side of the street.

Car doors slamming shut. Engines growling quietly. Dozens of beautiful, clean cars filling up with dozens of beautiful, clean people, carrying them safely back to their beautiful, clean houses.

Broom broom broom! For a minute the street is like the start of a motor-rally: the red and yellow and green and blue cars steering their shining bodies out of their parking-spaces and moving off down the street.

Only a handful of people are left behind now — and I on the pavement at a distance from them. I'm walking back, past the chapel again and into the small lounge of the Duke of Wellington.

As I lift my pint-glass to my cold lips my hands are shaking.

I light a cigarette and sit in the corner so that I can look up at the colour-television at the far end of the bar. I know nobody here. . . .

Dear old Ciardiff! In the cobbled streets of your docks Jimmy Driscoll was a barefoot nipper selling newspapers to earn a few pennies. He saw enough fisting and fighting outside the pubs of Butetown; that's where he learned the basics of his craft.

Today, in your grey docks they still talk about Driscoll and Wilde and Farr in their pubs as they drink scrumpy and dark, spitting and coughing their phlegm and fisting each other after stop-tap.

When I first came here from the green north I too used to go for a walk to the docks of an evening. There were more whores to be seen on the streets then.

"Willie, love, how's your middle leg tonight?" A toothy grin. A squaring of the bum in the tight skirt.

There was a strip-club, where the performers danced between the seats, close enough for you to count the stretch marks on their slack bellies. And in the Charleston women dressed as men kissing and embracing women dressed as women.

Yes, I saw many things down in Bute. But I never go there now. . . .

Hardly do I ever venture further than the city centre now. The streets of Splott and Roath are the only ones where I feel at home today. When I do go out, I walk the same pavements, drink in the same old pub, go to the same old cinema and have the same old experiences. My square mile. The familiar streets and the familiar thoughts. And all of it leading back to this shabby flat; to one unkempt bedroom, one untidy kitchen and one cold bathroom. To the black spot in the middle of the web. One insignificant little man and his pencil, his paper, his heavy belly, and his little window looking out over the narrow alley behind the home. The alley, and the rubbish bins, and the graffiti, and the stray cats. A spider watching the web attracting the dust. A king amid his brittle kingdom.

translated by Meic Stephens from *Bob yn y Ddinas* (1979)

ROBERT MINHINNICK

Dock

Greek and Irish, the shy Somalian
Make common language the city's nasal whine;
Brothers on the wharf as the cargoes
Come swinging overhead: oranges,
Iron, feldspar, grain, out of the sky
The world's tangible gift, a pittance now
As a shadow shift works the freighters,
Alexandra Dock reproachful with echoes
And this south part of the city an empty hold.

In the chart shop maps like dust sheets hang
From drawing boards, and a last technician
Traces blue fathom lines, as delicate
As webs, the irregular shelving
Of a coast eight thousand miles away.
His pen unlocks the sea. It roars in my head.
The compasses stride a continent
From the white edge of its desert coast
To the equatorial heart; a vessel
Manoeuvres into green Bahia,
Its cabins a dizzying fug of languages.

Walking the dock I find that world
Has vanished like a ship's brief wake.
Across the road the seaman's mission
Is a sour honeycomb of rooms,
The walls of dormitories marbled by the damp.
But where the money came ashore
The banks are moored, ornate as galleons,
All dark Victorian mortar
And the sudden frosts of engraved glass,
Their sooted corbels thrusting like
The jaws of Exchange millionaires.
Straight down to the water's edge
The road runs like a keel.

GORONWY JONES

Down and Out

I'm down and out. Been turned out of my flat, if that's what you'd call it. The sort of place where the bloody lot except the bog has been stuffed into one room. I had to pretend I was a student to get it when the dole boys stopped paying the hotel for me in Richmond Road. I was told by Frogit, the nice student, to go to some bird in the college, give her his name and ask for a cheap flat in Roath. Seven quid for one room is a bit of a dent but the place was handy for the Ely, the George, the Claude and the Crwys, so an alco like me wasn't complaining, was he?

To tell you the truth, I'm glad I left. Hellish funny people living there. The Paki next door wanting to borrow things all the time, and the closest thing you ever saw to a monkey living overhead and saying nothing except "Cool it man" every time I complained that his record-player was too loud.

"Bloody 'ell. Some of us got to work in the morning, mate," I said. "Not go to Joe Coral's like some."

But it was all right for him in that attic because the old bitch who owned the house lived on the ground floor and couldn't hear him. If she knew she would have been up there like a shot. No girls after ten. One bath a week after asking her to put the immersion on beforehand. No straining cabbage in the bathroom sink. There wasn't a sink in your bedroom, so if you were daft enough to boil cabbage I don't know where the hell you were supposed to strain it.

I'd had a hell of a good sesh on Saturday night, on a crawl with the lads, from the Claude to the Crwys and landing up in the Ely for singing and it was only natural for us to go down to Casa Martinez in St Mary Street to carry on. I'd better not admit that I haven't had much luck with the birds since I've been here in Cardiff. A bit too much of a scruff I think for these sedate little Welsh birds. But this bird came up to me while I was drinking wine with Stan Crossroads in the Casa.

"You want dancing?" she said to me.

A hellish funny way of saying it, I thought, but I'd be nuts to refuse. It was a slow tune and the bird clung to me like hell as we danced, and it suddenly dawned on me — Jesus, you're O.K. by here Gron! She was licking my red curls and saying she liked the kiss-curls behind my ears. I didn't know I had any. After one or two more glasses of wine and more kisses and cuddles, I told Stan I was leaving.

"Good luck," said Stan. "But you don't need much."

The bird was a nurse. Red hair like me. Birds of the same feather, aye? But she said she couldn't go back to the Heath at this time of night. They'd give her a hell of a ticking off. I knew the old bag in the house would be as sure as God to catch us, but where else could we go?

The next morning about seven o'clock, we crept out of the house and I was feeling great as I went to fetch the *News of the World* after putting the bird — Freeda her name was — on the bus. I'd managed to get past the guard at Ford Knox, aye? I didn't think any more about it, but when I came home from work on Monday evening, there she was — Mrs Wilcox — looking daggers at me at the foot of the stairs. Without uttering a word, she gives me a piece of paper.

"Notice to quit."

If I'd thought I'd hoodwinked *her*, I'd made a terrible mistake. Mrs Wilcox hasn't had a whole night's sleep since losing her husband four years ago. I felt sorry for her, to tell you the truth, and I used to bring her bits of spare carpet from work. Bits that would be all right to put on her hearth, aye. But all the Axminsters in the world wouldn't save the situation now.

Not only did she know that Freeda had been there all night, but Mrs Wilcox also used to go through the rooms of the four lads in her house every day, cleaning and emptying the bins and moving your things around. A good excuse to poke her nose in, I think. And what she saw on the chest-of-drawers made her really mad.

"I don't 'ave a son. But if I 'ad, I 'ope to God 'e wouldn't behave the way you do," is what I got.

And then I saw red. You've got to smile and pretend and suck the arse-holes of the toffs in Howells all day, and say Sir to the bosses you hate, but there's no chance in hell that anyone's going to tell me how to live in my own time, let alone go through my things and interfere.

"Stuff your notice," I said. "I'm going now."

And up I went to pack my cases and in a flea's wink I was walking over the threshold with a case in each hand.

"Merry Xmas to you too," I said, leaving the woman looking at me as if someone had stolen her cheese. And I bang the door as hard as I can.

It was only after I'd walked about a hundred yards down the street, still swearing and muttering under my breath that I realised what I'd done.

Where would I go? I've always said beer solves every problem so down I went by open- tap to the New Ely. Luckily, who was there as faithful as steel over his Guinness but Jero Jones the Welsh Learner.

"Hello, Gron," he said in Welsh. "You wanna pint? I am speaking splendidly now. Bad Welshman, who is thinking in English." He likes to get that over with before we have a proper chat in English. I told him my story and he agreed every now and again with his "Hope so" and "Can't do it." It was up your arse-hole Mrs Wilcox by nine and everyone in the Ely knew about my problem.

"I hope she chokes on her Horlicks this very night," I said.

"Hope so anyway. Hope so," said Jero.

"An old bag like that can't slag me off."

"Can't do it," said Jero. "Can't do it today."

"Come to our place tonight," said Frogit. "One of the lads will sure as God be staying with his bird." The lads live in Albany Road and are always taking in strays the likes of me. A boy from Brittany had been staying with Connolly for a month, came to Wales to dodge going into the army in France. His hair is down to his belly now, and I don't know how long it'll be by the time it's safe for him to go home.

Dai Shop, who's just got his licence back after being caught with the breathalyser at the Eisteddfod in Cricieth, also lives there and we all had a lift back with him in his car. Everyone except Frogit who's a bit of a ladies' man and courting some new bird every month.

"A student are you?" I said to the fifth lad in the car.

"Lord, no. I work in Saint Fagans," said the lad.

"Where?" I said.

"Welsh Folk Museum," the lad said.

"You know, Gron, where they re-build old houses from long ago," said Dai Shop, who's a teacher.

Not much the wiser, either.

We happened to go past Mrs Wilcox's street on the way home and I wind the window down, hang out of the car, raise two fingers and bawl like a wild man, "Stuff your bloody house, you bitch out of hell!" As if she could hear me.

The lads were laughing like piss and they laughed even more when I started to get sentimental later on and said if there were Good Samaritans today, they were them, giving a hand to lads like me when they're in trouble in Cardiff.

translated by Meic Stephens from Dyddiadur Dyn Dwad (1978)

JOHN TRIPP

Eglwys Newydd

The village is straddled on both sides
of a main road. Sometimes it shakes
from heavy transport and rock blasting.
A shabby brook runs through it,
mossed blue slate and cheapjack granite
of functional dwellings, crumbling since Victoria.
The most terrible accent in Wales
ends here, and the authentic one begins a mile away
in Tongwynlais. The pubs are full of silence.
Oliver Cromwell spent a night in a house
that is now a greengrocer's.
            It is one of those zones
for D.P.'s between England and Wales,
a Gaza Strip where nobody belongs.
If you asked them how their search
for identity was getting on, they'd look blank
or say you needed certifying
in the asylum up the road.
            It is one of the settlements
Rowland Lee would have praised,
being cleared of swarthy troublemakers
and neutered of Welshry. Dic Penderyn
would have yawned his head off.
            Loyalty to the crown
hangs in pastry and sweet shops
when the ladies and gentlemen come
to open things. Controversy is swept with fag-ends
into the gutter.
            I don't know why I live here.
I have been waiting a long time
for my visa to Tongwynlais.

157

GILBERT RUDDOCK

Wedding

In Mill Park, Cardiff

Cherry flowers in myriads
like confetti on the ground,
on lawn and earth and pathways.

As though there'd been
a wedding here.

Greenness and greyness bare
now together
under pink-white mantle
            of gentle falls.

But here there was no
trysting-place of boy and girl,
no splendid wedding-march.
Here there were no mother's tears
nor covenant of golden ring
and holy words.

Yet, there was a wedding
            for the thousandth time
in church of trees,
            in sound of leaves,
by the quiet old waters of Llechau brook.

Beauty was joined,
hue by hue,
to earth and dust and water's flow,
and in the joining
            every place
                  was changed.

On lawn and earth and pathways grey,
on dust and seat and water's way,
on branch of tree,
the joining of a miracle
    was gained in loss,
the unseen minister officiating
    without sound,
in perfect joy.

translated by the author

DUNCAN BUSH

Three Voices

EVELYN

I feel sorry for the bus. All the way out here it comes. And nobody hardly ever on it when it gets here. All round the estate it must come. Then here. This is the terminus. It stops here. But what for? Why do it bother? Nobody hardly ever comes here. Only on a Saturday or Sunday. And then, a lot of them got cars.

They call this place a home. But it's for people who haven't got one. When I was in the hospital at Llandough it was different. I used to like watching the buses come. I could see them from the ward or the day-lounge, down in the carpark there. Families, kids, they all used to come on the bus. It was like it was a proper trip out there for them. A day out. I know they was only coming to visit somebody in hospital, but to me it was always like it was a happy bus. Not sad. And really full, it used to be. Like they was all going down Lavernock or Barry Island or somewhere, or it might have been a Whitsun Treat. Like on the old charabancs.

Or am I getting it all mixed up? I do sometimes, I know.

And the kids. They always used to bring the kids. Children, grandchildren, all running about the ward. Of course, you can only keep them quiet for five minutes. They don't know what it is, a hospital. Or sickness. They don't know what it means.

But when you're in a place like that, that's what you want to see. A bit of young life. Not long faces, just sitting there with that bottle of Lucozade they brought. Or chatting about this and that like they can't wait for Sister to come through and tell everybody it's Time. Why do everybody always talk to you polite when you're in hospital? And in that quiet voice? It's not natural. It's like they was already sitting by you at the vigil.

I wish he was older, Dean. Because he still don't know who I am really, now. They don't at that age. He only knows his mother. He don't know I'm his Nana. He can't even say Nana yet, let alone understand it. Only, Dada, Dada. Everything's Dada to him, now. Kath says, It don't mean nothing, Mam. It's just a noise. They all say Dada when they're learning to talk. But it upsets me sometimes, when I see his little face. Because I know he haven't got a Dada really.

That don't matter, Kath always says. It don't matter if you don't know who your father is. Because starting a kid inside you is easy, she said. She said, Even having it, getting it out of you, is easy. It's the bringing it up for seventeen or eighteen years is the hard part. And that's all you need a father and mother for. And the ones who do that, they're your parents. And the ones who don't, aren't.

And I say, Easy? And I give a little, wavering laugh. Easy? If you only knew the years of that too, and the heartache.

But then, I could be like that Beattie, down the ward. She don't get nobody, no visitors. She can't have no family left. I feel sorry for her. She's a poor old dab.

Or that old Mrs Matthews. Particularly on a Sunday, when they get her smartened up, like all the rest. They got to do that, I know. So you can still have a bit of pride in yourself. So you still at least want to try to look nice. Mutton dressed as lamb is all it is, of course. And what's the point if you're just sitting there in the bed while everybody else got family round them? That's why she cries. It's terrible to listen to. Then they have to pull the curtain round her and try and quieten her down. Or she won't let Nurse make her up, she'll scream and fight. And she got a terrible mouth on her.

Keep your effing hands to yourself, she'll shout. I'm not a stiff yet. You can stuff your effing makeup.

But it's true. They do that to you when you're dead. To make you look a bit better, lying there. And it feels like that sometimes, when they put your nice bedjacket on you and some powder and do your hair for you. Or a bit of rouge, just to give you some colour in your cheeks. When you can't do it for yourself no more it's like you're already in your box. And you are, as good as.

What I can't stand is the way they never mention it. When someone, like, Passes On. They just pull the curtains round the bed. Then it's as if they sneak them out on a trolley in the night, like they was smuggling it out past you. As if you didn't know.

Then it's just the bed there, stripped. And sometimes it's as if you can't even remember who was in it, once they're gone.

It looks lovely out there now, all the daffs, and the grass. They keep it lovely, the grass. Sometimes we have our tea out there, if it's a nice day, and no wind.

But I do, I feel sorry for the bus. It's the only thing that makes me cry. All the way out from Town it comes. It turns round here. Then it'll just wait there. It's sad to think of it coming all the way out here when there's nobody on it. Like, it do try. But nobody hardly comes out this far. Not in the week. And nobody hardly gets on it, unless one of the nurses. Nobody goes from here. Not on the bus.

But sometimes I think I will. Like, it been coming here just for me, all this time. As if that's what it'll be like. Not like an ambulance, with them terrible black windows, or a big slow hearse. But on that orange bus. So you can look at houses, parks. And sit, with people.

He won't ever remember me, Dean.

MERVYN

I've lived in this city all my bleeding life, and I don't recognise it sometimes. Everywhere just gets shabbier and shabbier. It's like they're deliberately letting it fall down. It is, it's going to the dogs, this city.

I was down by Herbert Street last Sunday. I usually have a few pints in The Great Western of a Sunday night. But I had loads of time till seven o'clock opening, and it was a nice evening, so I thought, I'll walk in tonight. You know, down past the top of the Docks there. I don't suppose I'd been down that part for a year or two, Tyndall Street, Herbert Street, it's not a way I usually have call to go.

You ought to see it down there now. Herbert Street? It's all condemned. It's just a row of derelicts. It's a street going nowhere. Grass growing from the pavestones. Nettles in the rooms. It's like it's going back to jungle. Half the windows all bricked up. The other half stoned blind by kids. Corrugated sheeting on the doors, to keep the dossers out.

What I can't understand is how they can take all them houses off the market when there's people got nowhere to live? They're still sound as the dollar, most of them, you can see it. It don't make sense, to me.

I hate to see houses like that, just left to go to rack and ruin. You look at 'em and you think, Well, they're only ordinary terraced houses. But someone built them once. Somebody laid every brick. It was work for people. And people lived in them, for years.

You just have a look at all them skewback arches on the windows. It was more or less standard then, a skewback arch. You didn't have concrete lintels, not in them days. But you show me a bricklayer today who could put in a proper skewback arch for you. A skewback arch? They'd bloody laugh at you. You'd have a job to find one who could chance a guess on what it was.

But the saddest thing was at the one end on the street, where they'd already started the demolition. And you could see the dividing wall of the last house that had been knocked down. And you could see where the ceiling had been, and what wallpaper they'd had in the upstairs rooms. The one must have been a baby's bedroom, judging from the paper. And in the other, the bedroom at the front, you could even see on the wall a kind of lighter patch, a paler square, perfect it was, where a mirror or a picture must have hung. Hung there for years it must have. And I looked at it and I thought. Tomorrow morning, Monday, when they start the bulldozers again, that wall will be gone too.

I don't know what it is. But you see something like that, or you look at all them condemned houses and the work it took to build them, and it's enough to make you want to weep. And all this Council we got will ever do is to flatten them to build a carpark. Or sit on the land for a few years till the price is right, then sell it off to somebody like Julian Dodge, or Sir Julian he is now, to put another bloody office block on.

Like that Prudential Building. I can remember when they were building that, and they were talking about it in *The Echo* like it was a big thing for the city, Cardiff's Tallest Skyscraper or whatever. Skyscraper? More a concrete eggbox, nineteen stories high. With a red light on the top at night, and half the floors lit up on nothing.

I was walking past there the other night, and I was trying to remember what was there before it. And do you think I could? I've lived and worked in this city all my life, man and boy, and I couldn't remember what was there before.

But I suppose that's how it is. They knock something down, and it's as if it never been there. They put an eyesore like that up, that's half-empty and nobody even needs, and it's like it been standing there for ever.

They had a photo in *The Echo* the other night. Of Queen Street, some time in the Twenties. They been doing a bit of a series on Old Cardiff lately. The trams used to run down Queen Street in those days. I can remember the trams, from when I was a kid. St Mary Street was cobbled then. I could even remember some of the shops in the photo. They must have still been there when I was a boy.

But it's only when you look at an old photograph like that that you realise how much it have all changed. You don't even think of it if you're walking through the centre of Town, today. I suppose once it's gone it's gone. But you see an old photograph like that and you remember it, it all comes back.

Even the way they used to dress. Like everybody used to wear a waistcoat and a hat in them days. Even ordinary working men. My father always did. You'd never see my old man without a waistcoat on. And you could always tell a shonnie from the Valleys, by them big caps they used to wear. And the women would wear a hat. A woman wasn't dressed without a hat, not then. You can't believe it, looking at some of these young girls you see nowadays.

But you only remember it when you see one of them old photos. Because it was your everyday life, and it was like you never really noticed it, or thought about it anyway, till it was gone.

I suppose they're all gone now, all them on the pavements in that photo. Men, women, kids, the lot. The horses pulling that dray. They're in the ground. Well, some of the kids must still be alive.

There's always like a haze in them old photos, isn't there? You ever notice that? Like them old, grey Movietone newses. It's like you're always looking at things through a kind of mist.

But I don't know what it is. I know things change, but this city don't seem to have no character no more. Even the shopfronts. I mean, they was all small businesses or family firms in the old days. Like that one in the photo. Roberts, Gentleman's Outfitters. I think I can remember that being there. But you walk down Queen Street now and it's all Boots and C & A's and Marks and Spencer's. The Abbey National. Littlewood's. Barclay's Bank. It's all just standard frontages. You might just as well be walking down any street of shops in any other town in Britain. All plateglass and aluminium.

No, there's no real brickwork any more, let alone real bricklayers. It's all shopfitting jobs these days, or them precast units. You have a look at the centre of Town these days, and what is it? All traffic lights and shoe shops.

And you look at that Dodge Building or all them office blocks at night. And you think, That's what They're like. Big and empty. Exactly like the buildings they put up.

BILLY

Sometimes it's as if it have always been a bleeding Sunday in our house, ever since you was a kid. That smell of the Sunday dinner everywhere,

164

and it's like they still had 'Family Favourites' on the wireless, even. They haven't had that on for years, really. They must have took it off. But it's like you can still hear that theme tune. With A Song In My Heart. Da da da dadada dadada. Da da da dadada. They always seemed to have that on when we was having Sunday dinner, when the Old Lady was alive. And every Sunday it's like you can still bleeding hear it. It's the smell of the cabbage boiling or the meat, it is. And 'em all being there, waiting for their dinner. Like it haven't changed, nothing have changed, except for the Old Lady kicking it. As if all you ever did when you was a kid was wait for Sunday dinner. When you had any. And it's depressing, like them old snaps from their wedding in the drawer. They've gone all brown, like from being in the sun.

The Old Man brought this big joint home for today. Of beef. All wrapped up in this bloody piece of the newspaper.

"Where d'you get that?" Sheila said.

"It's first class meat," the Old Man said.

"I can see that," Sheila said. "That's why I'm asking where you got it." The Old Man just winked at me.

"It's a big piece," Sheila said. "I'll have to cook it all," she said, "or it won't keep. It's a pity we can't freeze some of it."

It was a big piece of beef all right. It must have been *that* long, I'm not kidding. It was like in a roll, and all corded round the fat.

"Well," the Old Man said, "it was either this or a sheep's head. The feller said, 'Just leave the eyes in when you cook it. It'll see you through the week.' 'No,' I told him. 'I'll have the piece of beef this time'."

Silverside, the Old Man said it was. I'm sick of it already, just from the smell of it cooking all through the house, and it being Sunday. And I was hanging about in the kitchen watching Sheila take it out the oven and tip the tray, and all the brown fat off it run in the corner. And she poured it on the roast spuds with a spoon, and it was hissing and spitting like a cat. It was all sunny outside, but you couldn't see out of the window in the kitchen because it was all steamed up from the vegetables on the stove.

Then our Tommy come down.

"All right, Bill?" he said.

"Get away," I said to him.

I hate it when he messes up my hair like that. Of course, he thinks it's clever. He pretended he had to wipe his hands off down his jeans.

"Sheila," he said. "Billy been at the lard again. You got enough left to cook us a dinner with?"

"It's not lard," I said. "It's Brylcreem. If you want to know."

"Not lard?" he said.

He sniffed his hands.

"You sure?"

Then he went in the doorway and had a deep breath, smelling the cooking.

"What's for dinner?" he said.

"Wait and see," Sheila said.

Tommy come in the back room after me, and sat there. He lit a fag.

"All down the club are they?" he said.

"Yeah," I said.

I combed my hair again in the mirror above the mantelpiece. He sat there for a bit, with this fag.

"Look at that smoke," he said. "It must be really still in here, the air. No draught, like."

The smoke was hanging in the air, like in layers, almost. It was blue in the shadow and all bright grey where the sun was on it.

I think it was the sun coming in the window that was making me feel sick. It's always like that, on a Sunday. Sun day: that's what it means. I prefer the winter, when you can sit in front of the fire on a Sunday afternoon. The fire was lit, but it looked dead. You know, where the sun was on it. It ruins a fire, the sun. And it was shining in on the back of the flue too, and all the soot on the bricks was brown with it, and like a fur. And Sammy's fur did use to be like that. It was as black as anything when he was a young dog. But when he got old it went all brown when he was lying in the sun.

Then Sheila came in for a minute.

"If you're going down the club, " she told Tommy, "tell 'em not to be so bloody late this week. It'll be done for half past two."

Tommy yawned.

"I dunno," he said, like he was too tired to move. "I might just have a drink in the house instead. Any of that whisky left?"

Sheila laughed.

"You're joking," she said. "The Old Man seen that off. Anyway," she said, "if they're not here by half past two, I'm putting their dinners up. They can have it when they come in. It won't be my fault if it have all dried up in the oven. I'm starving," she said. "You hungry, Billy?"

"No," I said. "I feel a bit sick."

"Aw," Tommy said. "Poor little Billy feel a bit sick, do he?"

166

In that stupid voice he always puts on, like talking to a baby. I went out the back. I couldn't stand it in there no more, not with him there. But it was as bad out the back. Just them hens scraping in the dirt behind all that old leaning wire. And all them old cabbage stumps still in the ground. You think the Old Man would pull 'em up and burn 'em on the bonfire or something. Instead of just leaving 'em standing there all scruffy and yellow and scaly, like a chicken's leg.

I hate this house. And I hate 'em all being here. I wish they'd all just go down the club and bloody stay there, of a Sunday. Not to mention 'em coming in on a Saturday night at all hours, waking me up. It's always the bleeding same, with Cliff and Tommy. They don't think they've had a Saturday night out unless they've fallen down in public twice and shat their pants or something. Then they comes in the bedroom at one or two o'clock, staggering about the place and breathing heavy. Or there's Cliff lying there, like last night, talking to himself like Clint Eastwood in the films. Effing and blinding, beating people up under his breath.

I do. I hate 'em. The pair of 'em. Especially when they're in that state, and having to sleep in the same room with 'em. And it's always worse on the weekend. Particularly on a Saturday night. And then the Sunday, with 'em all here, hanging around the house. They never go nowhere on a Sunday, just down the club at dinnertime. Then they'll eat their dinner quick and grab the two good chairs, with their afters on their knees, to watch the darts or something. When they know I been looking forward to 'Bonanza'.

Why don't they get bloody married? I mean, he's thirty bloody two, our Tommy. You'd have thought he would have found some silly bugger to have married him by now. The twins did. They're gone, Bryn and Vince, they're damn well out of it.

I'd go somewhere myself, just to get away from 'em. But where is there, on a Sunday afternoon? There's nowhere open. Even the pictures don't open till gone five, on Sunday.

There was some little kids playing football on the waste ground over the back. Darren from down the road and his mate. He's really blonde, that little Darren. Anyway, I hung about there for a bit, watching 'em. In case they miskicked or anything, and I had the chance to kick it back. They think you're a bit funny if you try and play with 'em. You know, if you're a grown up. So in the end I thought I better go back in anyway.

"Everything's just about done," Sheila said.

Tommy wasn't in the back room. He must have gone down the club

167

after all.

Though, it was funny, that fag smoke was still there, hanging in the room. It like veered away a bit when I blew at it.

"Well," Sheila said, "I'm not waiting any longer for 'em. I'm sick of this happening every bloody week. I told 'em half past two. They'll have to have theirs out the oven."

She was draining the cabbage water off, into the sink. It was a proper green.

"I better save a cupful of this for the Old Man, I suppose," she said.

The Old Man drinks it. For the iron, he reckons. When we was kids he always used to try and get us to, as well. But none of us ever would. Me, I always have hated cabbage.

I was just mooning about in the kitchen there, watching her while she was doing things. But Sheila's all right. I don't mind Sheila being there. She wrapped a cloth round her hands and took the meat out.

"It've shrunk a bit," she said. "That's because I never had no foil. But it's a lovely piece of meat. I suppose next week it'll be duck again. Duck under the bleeding table."

Then she had to go and sharpen up the knife on the outside step, to cut it. And I was watching her hand going to and fro with it, turning the blade over on the stone.

"It's a dead loss this knife," she said.

Sheath sheath sheath, it went on the stone. That was the noise it made. But it wasn't a sheath knife. It was a proper carving knife. The blade was thin in the middle from being sharpened on the edge of that stone step.

Then Sheila come in the kitchen again with the knife and cut a little bit of the brown outside off the end of the meat, to try it.

"Here you are, Billy." she said.

I made a face at it.

"I don't want none," I said. "And I don't want no dinner either. I feel sick."

So she ate it instead.

"That's always the best bit," she said. "Cook's privilege. Though a glass of sherry first would have been nice as well. Open one of them windows, will you," she said. "Let the steam out a bit."

The window panes was all grey with the steam. I had a look out the back, but Darren must have gone off home. I drew a face on one.

from *Hinterlands* (an unpublished novel)

GILLIAN CLARKE

Cardiff Elms

Until this summer
through the open roof of the car
their lace was light as rain
against the burning sun.
On a rose-coloured road
they laid their inks,
knew exactly, in the seed,
where in the sky they would reach
precise parameters.

Traffic-jammed under a square
of perfect blue I thirst
for their lake's fingering
shadow, trunk by trunk arching
a cloister between the parks
and pillars of a civic architecture,
older and taller than all of it.

Heat is a salt encrustation.
Walls square up to the sky
without the company of leaves
or the town life of birds.
At the roadside this enormous
firewood, elmwood, the start
of some terrible undoing.

GILLIAN CLARKE

Missa Pontcanna

Forty years confined
in the sisterhood of silence. Noise to her
was chink of rosary, footfall
on gravel in a walled garden,
trapped song of blackbird
the hour before Angelus.

In a world unimagined before today
she shared the night with a crowd gathering
in darkness like a great migration,
the dawn moon dissolving,
the rose-window of the rising sun.

She has known in one dazzling day
circus and seaside, fair-day and birthday,
oratorio, picnic, holy day, holiday,
crowd, Kyrie, caritas, caru,
and a Pope behind glass, his smile distant
after television's intimacy.

First sight of the world —
a hundred thousand picnic by a river,
the old faint in the heat, the young
sunbathe profanely, diving for joy in the Taff.
First sound after silence a crowd's roar
under yellow flags like barley in wind.

Catching her patience the Taff loiters
in shadow, falls in a wimple of pleats
over Blackweir counting its prayer on stones.
Dizzy, sunburnt, as at the close of any
secular day, they queue for the bridge.
Thunder growls and the rain begins.

Something is over. In the cell of herself
the day stores its honey and an image
of the world for whose salvation
she tells and tells her beads.

JOHN TRIPP

On Hayes Island

Young miners down for the day
sit apart, huddled like a cabal;
for some reason they remind me
of those Red sailors who mutinied
long ago.
      Under a gunmetal sky
the pigeons gather for crumbs
as I freeze at a tin table
above the public convenience,
waiting for something to turn up,
feeling far from debonair
in the black ice of a scimitar winter.

This is Cardiff's Montmartre
without the wine and conversation.
You can buy wine from a store
and drink it unmolested on a bench,
but you can't buy conversation.
It is a rendezvous for the impoverished
pockets of want that dwell on the brink.

Listless, I tap my shoe
on the bottle-glass grid of the bog roof
and watch the fine women of South Wales
shuttling across the Hayes.
They look as if they're going somewhere,
serious, with bulging shopping bags.

At dusk, the clock on St John's Church
strikes five as a drizzle begins
and the shutters go up on the tea shack.
By now, even the pigeons have had enough
and fly away to Splott. . . .

from 'Life Under Thatcher' (1985)

172

OLIVER REYNOLDS

Daearyddiaeth

The land was always worked.
It was what you lived on.
So the feelings were strong:
The land was in your heart;
The land was underfoot.

It's still farmed, flat and hill,
Some of it good, some bad.
Cash crops may oust *hiraeth*,
But it's still praised: *Gwlad, gwlad*
With the ball hanging air.

And many of the poems
Carry the smack of loam,
In books of earthy style
Whose pages you leaf through
Like someone turning soil.

It wasn't long before
Love and the land were one.
Sweethearts had their contours
While streams grew feminine.
Desire and greening joined.

The genre pullulated.
Venus came on vernal.
The body pastoral
Was sung or lamented
As was Arthur's, grass-graved.

What thought of city loves?
Hamlet's country matters
Aren't foreign to the town:
We've enough to ensure
Cupid stays urban.

173

Poets of the precincts
Lacking parallels
Instinct with the instincts
Should exchange Arcady
For the brick of Cardiff.

Fingers that divagate
Along the vertebrae
Assume Sanquahar Street,
Sesquipedalian
Way to the timber yards.

The gasworks surplus burns
Behind Jonkers Terrace.
Wind flutes and twists the flame,
The gold column broken
Into plaits and tresses.

The path to Thornbury Close
Dwindles into Thornhill
Where tight dawn is seeping
Bit by bit into day:
Someone slowly waking.

At the side of the path
Is an old lamp-standard
Whose bulb is lit but pale
Above the base's stamped
And simple avowal:

D. Evans   Eagle Foundry
Llandaff 1911.

JAN MORRIS

Fine Enough in its Way

Cardiff, however, is the capital of Wales, and Cardiff is where the TV studios are, and Cardiff Arms Park, and the Welsh National Opera, and the *Western Mail*, and in Cardiff the chocolate-voiced all-but-English businessmen drive about in their Mercedes, or scoff at the Welsh language in lounge bars ('Though mind you, I'm as good a Welshman as any one of them . . .') while their wives practise their Knightsbridge idioms over calorie-light lunches with Perrier. Cardiff docks are quiet these days, and hardly a ton of coal passes down the railway tracks from one year to the next, but the city has bounced back from successive depressions, all the same, in a heady effervescence of opportunism, fuelled frequently with nepotism and publicity campaigns. Cardiff is Post-Industrial Wales, living by its wits and its service trades: and less than a dozen miles from the acheing sadnesses of the Rhondda, where a way of life, a language and a faith were still wasting away in redundancy and unemployment, in 1983 a third of this city voted Conservative.

Bright, brash, profitable, clever and cosmopolitan though it is, Cardiff is weak on *presence*. It tries to be a national capital, but it remains a witness to the political impotence of Wales, and to the innately centrifugal instincts of the Welsh. In the days when it was the Marquis of Bute's coal port it had a functional cohesion, suspended between the poles of docks and castle: now it lies there more indeterminately, weakened by parks and demolition areas, with no powerful focus or density of form. The castle is still there, of course, and with its great gates and towers, and its long surrounding walls strewn with sculptured lions, bears, monkeys and dragons, provides as splendid and unexpected a centre-piece as any city could want. But it is only a show-place now, not a power-house, just as the glorious old commercial centre of Butetown is half moribund, half self-consciously resuscitated, and is surrounded by a waste of apparently abandoned developments. Solid bourgeois shopping streets, where once the trams and hansoms lurched, have been prettily converted into pedestrian precincts with potted shrubs and tessellated pavements: Tiger Bay is all gone, all its squalors, sprees and dangers, and down at the docks, where the colliers filled their holds to that clang and clatter of the tippers, a Museum of Maritime Affairs has been opened in a gaily done-up warehouse.

Superimposed upon it all, too late perhaps for conviction, are the institutions of a capital. There is a national concert hall (built partly with funds from the European Community), there is a national stadium, and a school of music and drama; and at a confusing angle to the lie of the city, in the first half of this century there arose a monumental centre of officialdom — a long grass rectangle surrounded by buildings, the National Museum and the Welsh Office and the University and the City Hall and the County Offices and the Temple of Peace and Health — imposing portentous structures, ornate with texts and statuary in the Washington or Canberra mode, with a national war memorial in the middle and flags flying here and there. It is fine enough in its way, and impresses foreigners expecting only coal-grimed slums and dereliction: but it is hardly Cardiff really, and for that matter hardly Wales.

from *The Matter of Wales* (1985)

TONY CURTIS

Thoughts from the Holiday Inn

for John Tripp

"When you're dead, you're bloody dead."
We both liked the punch of that one, John, said
Ten or more years ago by an author breaking
Through his fiction, kicking the rules, risking
All our willing disbelief to shock through
To the truth. B.S. Johnson, that sad and tortured man, knew
The whole thing to be by turns a joke, by turns the need
To love each other into something close to sense. We bleed,
John, we bleed, and time bleeds from our wrists.
Your death was shocking, and tidies up another lovely, angry (when
        pissed),
Poet of a man, who would not, for anyone, be tidied into respectability
Longer than an evening, or his allotment in some anthology.
There's too much to be said, by too many, too soon.
But from this lunchtime watering place, this unlikeliest of rooms,
Spare me the modest time and space — by Christ, you've enough
Of both in death, old mate — to work things out, sound off —
About the months you've missed, the months that we've missed you.
You'd have seen this place go up, the skyline that you knew
Transformed, jagged, blocked as urban planners brought rationality
To what the Coal Century had grown and shaped to the Taff's estuary.
We've needed you here, John, thrusting out your neck and stroking the
        chin
From a classy, fraying shirt to show the distain we hold these people in,
These late-comers to a country and a nation in a mess.
They've given us the bum's rush today, John, I must confess.
We checked out the place for next year's Literature Festival
And sponsorship. As far as we could tell
It was a waste of time, for any management
Who'd given Sickle-Cell Research the thumbs down were clearly bent
On profit, and to hell with charity, never mind cultural P.R.
Well fed and disappointed, we returned to the bar.
Still, they'd named the two big function rooms, the 'Dylan Suite'

And 'Gwyn Jones Room'. "Don't know him," said the manageress, with complete
Honesty. "He's one of our Academy's most distinguished senior members,"
I said, and thought, We do no more than blow upon the embers,
We scribblers who'd want to claim
That everything in Wales for praise or blame
Is brought to life and fact and mythical creation
By that writerly mix of ego and the grasp of a tradition.
What use we prove, the weight of the world gives us, if any,
Is likely to be cheap and grudging, no more than a blunt penny
Flung to shut our mannered, metred whining,
Then, later, taken up again shining
From the rubbing our tongues and lives impart.
I hear you answer, John, "It's a start, boy, some sort of bloody start."
John, further down the Hayes, now I think of you, haunting those benches
And passing a coffee or the length of a fag below the rich stenches
From Brains's brewery snugged in behind the Morgan Arcade.
As the big internationals move in and build and build the shade
And sunlight shift position down the city's roads.
In spruced-up Bute (re-named, as Tiger Bay encodes
A docklands past we'd best forget or sanitise
In tarted-up pubs or tree-lined low-rise
Flats — *The Jolly Tar* or *Laskar's Close*)
The men who clinch the deals, the gaffers, the boss
With the tax-free Daimler, the Series Seven,
Square out the mazy city into real estate concepts, proven
Returns for their money. They are gilt-edged applicants
For Euro-funds, Welsh Development grants.
This hotel is for the likes of them. It stretches eye to eye
With the brewery's silver funnel, two hundred bedrooms in the sky
Starting at fifty quid the night. "Fat cats," I hear you say,
"And that's before your breakfast. Stuff the fucking pool, O.K."
Tax payer's rage? John, even you, an occasional connoisseur
Of hotel fitments and glimpses of the soft life, would incur
A gullet-sticking at this pricy junk, mock-Grecian style
Arches, columns, thick marble-facings done in tiles,
Plush, deep divans around an open fire beneath a metal canopy,
Surrogate logs you'd hardly warm your hands upon. You'd see

178

Beyond, the indoor pool, functional, gaunt,
More marble, sharp angles with, each end, broken columns to flaunt
The facile version of classic decor money'll buy
And set down in a city anywhere, across a sky
Or ocean. Continent to continent there must be travellers
Who need the reassurance of such nondescript pools and bars,
To step off the plane or train, taxi down concrete tracks
To what the Telex reservation guarantees predictable: stacks
Of credit-cards accepted, pool-side temperature just O.K.
An in-house movie they choose and relay
To each room in American or English — God forbid
The native patois — (*These people down here, the Welsh — did*
You say — a language all their own — an ancient tongue?
— King Arthur — well, I saw a movie when I was a kid, sung
The songs all that summer — Dannie Kaye — got it!)
John, what kind of progress is all this shit?
They took the coal-miners and put 'em in a coal museum:
And the people drove down, coughed up three quid ten just to see 'em.
Tourists one-nighting en route the Beacons, Bath or Ireland:
"Cardiff — what's that?" " The airport . . . it's halfways there. I planned
To break the trudge from Heathrow." And what of the locals?
Lunchtimes bring yuppies of both sexes, the gals
Waft in like *Cosmo* covers, the men have knife-
Creased casuals, hook their index fingers through the keyrings of life.
And there's the mid-day nibblers, women past their prime
But dressed to the nines and painted, passing the time
Between Howells' upholstery and Hones and Jones with a small gin
And sandwich triangles of horseradish and smoked salmon,
Piquant, hardly fattening. Their cigarette smoke curls
Away with the suggestion of rope, these former good-lookers, girls
Who, thirty years before, bagged a man of promise or means
And moved up, to Cyncoed, out to Lisvane, a pool, lawns
Done by a man who brings his own machine and strips
His shirt in the long afternoons. They tip
Him with the last cut of September.
Their husbands are on the board and successfully bored. "Remember,"
They'd say, "when we had that little detached in Newport,
And we'd spend Sundays, you mowing and me trimming." "I've fought
Hard to get this far, and Christ, there's times I wonder,

179

What for? What have we got? Where's it gone? Just blunder
On to the next rung, dinner party, contract, barbeque."
"Love, you're working too hard. Is the company proving too much for
    you?"
John, excuse this indulgence, that clumsy fiction, it's no digression,
I'm still concerned to understand progression.
When working-class is all you've known
These rich fish cruise by bright-coloured (if overblown)
Distracting — but these too are tenants of the pool
You plunged your wit and pen into. Fool
No-one was your aim, and at last came the anger of *Life Under Thatcher*.
But winos in the Hayes betray a watcher
Who'd sum up the whole state of things in verses.
It's too easy to shoot off steam in curses
That pepper the mark but fail to penetrate.
Guys with real assets, clever portfolios, are immune to street hate;
They justify themselves in terms of respectability, vision, advancement.
The world's an oyster if you lift your nose off the pavement.
They've bought themselves out of the firing line.
Windows purr close, revs slipping the motor into fifth gear, it feels fine
To loosen out along the motorway — weekends in Pembs
Or, turning right, over the Bridge, a trim two hours to dine by the
    Thames.
No-one's rooted anymore, John, as you must have known —
"The old man" coming to smith in Taffs Well in the '30s where you'd
    grown
Up Welsh, not Cornish like him, in all but the language.
(The wounding of that loss, it seems, no achievements can assuage.)
And, because of that, confused, determined and concerned
As the rest of us, excluded from the *Gorsedd* but feeling you'd earned
The right to sound off for this Wales — Taffs and Gwerin,
To voice the peculiar place of the eighty per cent. The din
Of justified protest settled after '79 — Welsh cheque books, Channel
    Four.
The nationalist drummings the Sixties saw you working for
You realised later were too easy, too raw. Like R.S.
You loved the country with a passion, an anger, but the less
Misty, period-costume work will surely prove the best,
The more enduring; real poetry "welcoming the rough-weather guest".

John, I would rather have seen your ashes ebb from Barafundle
Bay. That grey day at Thornhill we watched your coffin trundle
Behind the curtains to the kind of anonymity
You'd rail against for other "botched angels", losers we
Turn away from, society's mistakes, the hard-done-to,
Underdogs you wanted to feel close to.
The glow of a cupped-hand fag was light enough to draw
You to some alley, a derelict huddled there against a door,
One of the Hollow Men, a voter with no vote
Wrapped in old woollens, *Echoes* stuffed inside an overcoat.
"Cold enough, butt, eh? on the street. Here, have yourself a cuppa.
Take care, old fella, and watch out for the copper.
Those bastards aren't for the likes of us,
They don't give a tinker's cuss
As long as things stay down and quiet, and everything's neat.
You and me'll keep to the shadows, butt, and stay light on our feet."
I've a feeling poetry's not the thing most apt
To dissect society, or politicise an audience one imagines trapped
In wilful ignorance, lobotomised by the trashy press,
Disenfranchised by the soapy box, seduced by the caress
Of the goodish life in the second half of this softening century.
You, fellow sprinter, took your chance through readings — could be
Five or fifty listeners, in club, gallery, college, school.
But articles in the London nationals, plays on the t.v. as a rule
Work most action, albeit short-lived. We
Poets light shower-burning fuses or rockets you see
Flash and quickly fade as the moment's charged
And spent. John, you saw the first decade of this city enlarged,
Pulled into the dream-shape someone thought we needed.
At fifty-nine who's to say you'd not changed things, not succeeded
In stirring up whatever stuff this corner of the pool had in suspension?
Talk of booze, too little care taken of yourself, prevention
Of the heart's explosion that took you in the early hours
With McGuigan's fight won and the tele drizzling showers
Of grey flakes down its mute screen,
Won't bring you back. You slid away. The barely-tuned machine
Packed up. Unlike Dylan, no insult to the brain, John. Often we'd talk
Of going to the States, whistle-stopping, the Chelsea in New York,
Our tour for the Yanks, I could have rigged.

Yes, if I'd pushed it, we two in tandem could have gigged
Over there. Like a lot of the others, I chickened out, I suppose.
Pembrokeshire a couple of nights — you with no change of clothes,
Just a battered attaché, poems, toothbrush, fags —
Was the limit of my stamina for your ways. Memory drags
Such petty guilts to the fore.
Though I treasure and feed off that reading we did on the man o' war,
Reluctant sailors pouring export ale down us
To forestall the poetry (they did) drown us
With hospitality in the middle of Fishguard harbour
Until we staggered past the missiles in her belly's store
Up to the frigate's redundant forward gun-turret, officers dressed
In cummerbunds, and elegant women. The talk was veiled, but impressed
Words like 'Responsibility', 'Capability' and 'Global role'. "Yes, but
What do you do with all this training? All the missiles, shit-hot
Fire-power?" I remember, he answered you with, "We can blow
    Fishguard
Away with each one, you know. We are, I suppose, a 'hard
Fist gloved by our democratic masters'." John, before the evening ended
You topped that with a poem scribbled on a cigarette pack. We
    descended
A precarious ladder to the launch with those lines of his and yours sinking
Into the night. And now, a decade later, the story has a ring
Any writer could tune. Perhaps that's what your Sandeman Port
    inquisitor
Pointed to — after the jaunts and applause, the writer's for
Filling the void, putting structure into space, a kind of race
Against apathy and oblivion. Too grand, you say, too heroic? Let's face
It, John, we've both indulged in our 'intervals of heat'
On the page and off. Both been chilled by the thought one couldn't beat
The odds — stuck in Wales, chiselling verse, weak in the flesh.
We're out on the edge of the world's concern, no Wall St, no Long Kesh.
Unless the challenge here is also to connect — radar dishes at Brawdy,
Hinkley over the water, Trawsfynydd, the poison brought in on our sea.
An *Anglo*, dipped in England's sewer should still produce the goods.
Albeit in invisible ink / on dissolving paper . . . one loads
The futile quarto, pushes it out to travel or sink.
Standing here before the Holiday Inn, and its shiny 0-3-0, I think
How my grandfather, before the Great War, shunted down to Wales on

the G.W.R.
How arbitrary one's identity is: with voice and gesture we are
Challenged to make sense of where and what we find ourselves. No
Border guards patrol the Dyke, no frontier seals us in at Chepstow.
Did you really ever want that, John, seriously?
From here I have to question that stance. Were you quite as you appeared
    to be?
This locomotive worked the sidings in Cardiff and the junction,
Was scrapped at Barry and now is made to function
As an image of our hard-bitten history. *9629*, freshly painted green and
    black,
Her valves de-gutted, holds to her half-dozen yards of track:
No driver on the footplate, no steam, no destination,
This featureless hotel its final station,
Under the flags of Canada, Commerce and the Dragon.
I turn around. On the island in the Hayes a wino tilts his flagon
And light flashes from the moment.

GWYN THOMAS

A Fine, Strong City

The Normans came in from the sea and coal came down from the hills. The coal made even more money than the Normans, and a gaggle of cottages around a huge castle became a city which has at last managed to get itself recognised as the capital of Wales.

Its claims to pre-eminence are challenged by townships whose title deeds to being the capital are often inscrutable. One will assert that John Elias preached his longest sermon there, and wants some compensation even though it is a hundred and thirty years late. Another will claim to have staged the only Eisteddfod in which the winning tenor, by vocal force alone, kept the canvas wholly clear of the marquee poles. In a third one, one of Wales's early harassed princes, who emerges from history books as having been almost continuously on the run, paused and uttered a prophecy of ruin before going on to the next leg of his unhappy marathon. Our annals are full of doom-laden utterances, and they have kept up a pretty steady level of accuracy.

But Cardiff, to all but a few Welshmen, is the city. The whole sweep of the south-east Glamorgan landscape around it has a magic pattern. Northward from Cardiff, like the fingers of a bruised hand, shoot the great valleys that would have produced, given a little more attention and a little less rain, a culture of brilliant vitality. One half of Cardiff is the life that streams into it from the northern hills. For millions of children from the Rhondda Cardiff has been the nerve-end of all delight, the glare at the end of the tunnel, their first contact with a well-lit urbanity, the first visible evidence of wealth and ease.

For one who lives in Cardiff but who once made his first journey there down the railway that rushes through Porth and Pontypridd, the walk along Queen Street towards the castle can never be undertaken without a tremor of expectation. The sensation is helped by the fact that Cardiff is a city of the most inexplicable draughts. Around the General Station in particular, a family of winds has got itself stuck and there has been no one to show them the way out. They reproduce in their tempo and sound the tumultuous anxieties of the travellers inside the station.

It is quite a place, that main terminal in Cardiff. South Wales has been one of the classic lands of emigration. If a South Walian wants to look at his motherland he has to keep turning, for his brothers are everywhere. And it is on the platforms of Cardiff General that the shattered heart reassembles. One could not count the number of times one has seen two or more Welshmen come out of their train, and as they hurry on to the next stage of their journey, one hears them shout, "See you in Cardiff the day of the match. In the Park, the Queen's, the Grand, the Royal.' Or whatever bar or cinema front takes their fancy.

Cardiff is the settled Zion of the Welsh Israelites. A face you may have glimpsed in Maerdy, Ammanford, Treharris, Blaencwm, and thought never on this earth to see again, be sure that one winter's afternoon it will come again into view in the swift river of people that flows down Quay Street towards the gates of the Arms Park.

The Arms Park is the great shrine. The memories of the great games that have been played there have been worn as smooth as pebbles by every talking group in the taverns and clubs of the region. They have become, for many, a sort of ritual incantation which has come close to ousting the theological and political jousts of yesteryear. Men who were not born at the time will come to blows over who scored the try that beat the All Blacks in 1905. The only person in the nook who was really there says nothing. After thirty years of recounting the epic he shut up for good in 1935.

If you have that over-forty feeling and are quietly dusting your policies, come and stand in a capacity crowd at the Arms Park when they sing one of the great hymns. The sadder the hymns the better, because that allows the boys to dig deep for their harmonies. It is typical of us that if the hospitality is lavish, we are often married and buried to the rhythm of the same superb graveside chants. At the Arms Park it is like being caught up in some mighty natural force; it gives you a taste of what it must have been like to be caught up in the fierce, hypnotic frenzies of tribalism.

Even notoriously discourteous spectators, whose banter has peeled the paint off the old stand, have been so overwhelmed by this experience they have gone through the entire match glassy-eyed and opening their mouths only to advise the referee to wear longer knicks when the colder weather comes. But our choral tradition is crumbling somewhat. The vast anthems of yearning melancholy are often displaced by flimsier tunes, and the folk on the two-bob bank, being chilled, sing a brisker measure than the cosier choristers in the stands, and the first group can often be well into the third verse when the rearguard is still edging its way out of the overture. This, in so vocally conscious an area, is going to cause some

185

heavy neuroses. But even now, on form, the lads can blow a hole in heaven and reduce a complete military band to the status of a solitary fifer on an upland.

The speaking voices of this city fascinate. The immigrant half, the visitors from the hills, speak with a singing intonation, as if every sentence is half-way into oratorio, the vowels as broad as their shoulders. The Cardiff speech, a compound of the native dialect and a brand of High Bristolian, gives an impression of a worldly hardness. They speak of 'Cairdiff', 'Cathays Pairk', and for a long time it is not amiable to the ear. There is an edge of implied superiority in it to the rather innocent and guileless openness of the valley-speech. As you move towards the docks, an area still on the dark and ghetto-like side, you hear the high, soft speech of a hundred tongues from Africa and the East, or perhaps from the lips of a child born into the docks, an enchanting mixture of Somerset, Madagascar and Pontllanfraith.

The docks do not live as abundantly as they did. There is always a little blood on the moon in the economic life of this zone. The hills, if you count out some pretty active patches of subsidence in the valleys, are fairly steady, but industrial trends have been on the jumpy side. The stress on coal, as we see it now, was a deadly, paralysing truss. The truss is broken but cramps linger. The rise of Cardiff as a port is one of the great dramatic tales of British commercial history. Between 1890 and 1920 so much coal left these wharves, we marvel that the world is ever cold or that we have anything left to stand on.

The dynasty of Cardiff tycoons, Lord Glanely and the rest, hard and resolute as the crews they sent out to the oceans, set their mark upon the city. Cory Hall commemorates one of the greatest coalowners. The lovely Temple of Peace stands witness to the zeal of Lord Davies of Llandinam, who put his fortune to work in the cause of international unity and peace. It was a relatively simple world they lived in. A hustling commerce had coal as practically the single currency. The British merchant marine was supreme.

We know what happened to coal. Markets shrank as conflict in the coalfield grew. We, who knew the coal valleys as children during the 'twenties, saw so many long stoppages of work we almost regarded life as a lunatic escapade in which normality just dropped flat on its face every whipstitch. "If you are good you can have an idle pit for Christmas," was one of the merrier proverbs of the time. There were local pigeons that tried to shed their homing instinct before each big race. The mansions of

186

Cardiff's docksmen edged into a sad dusk as flats and offices. History will dismiss the whole thing as a growing-pain. Today, the Cardiff docks, like the rest of South Wales, are finding their way to a more varied and reliable activity. In the city's centre is a patch of noble amenity in marble and granite. Wealth did not come too long before civic pride here, and there is an Athenian grace about the group of buildings, the County and City Halls, the Museum, the Law Courts, that extend the castle's dignity on the city's northern side. Among the buildings are bits of memorial statuary. To the artist they bring no comfort, and to the social historian they are odd. The men remembered were, without doubt, wise, brave or rich, but a bronze frock coat, considered as deathless art, does not even get started.

South Walians are proud of this city centre. The museum, in itself and in the things it encloses, is a place of miraculous beauties. South Walians generally point to this parkland of gracious architecture with a somewhat angry pride. Angry because their valleys are a syllabus of every error that can make human dwellings of a repellent unworthiness. Long streets laid out like grey bruises on the soaked and puzzled hills; places of public assembly apparently designed by sinister misanthropes to keep the public dispersed. Let the valley dweller, or for that matter a resident of Bute Street or Grangetown, step forth from Kingsway and head towards the University College buildings, and he will have intimations of a lush and laundered future.

The modern history of Cardiff's castle has a fair number of ironical turns. These Welsh castles never fail to give the historical fancy a kick. Most of them are a low, defensive mutter in an alien, hating land. Time and ruin have brought them a pathos of peace. But the steady residence of the Butes in this pile has given it a lived-in, manorial touch. It now belongs to the Cardiff Corporation.

The Third Estate crowds in to stroll and glance at a shilling a head, bemused at being on the domestic hearth of the power against which they have been waging a stubborn rearguard action for the last nine hundred years. A ghastly blockage, castles.

Part of the castle is now a College of Music and Drama. The visitor can listen simultaneously to the wailing ghost of Robert of Normandy, who spent twenty years here in a type of deep well, and the uncertain sounds of art in its rough stage.

The rebuilt section of the castle, through which tourists are conducted in gasping groups (astonishment and stairs activate the gasps), is a nineteenth-century flourish of triumphant wealth. The Chaucer room, a bed- chamber with a conical ceiling made up of illustrations in coloured glass of Chaucer's tales, in which some privileged insomniac might well have dropped off while counting Canterbury lambs. There is a room designed to reproduce the reclining chamber of a harem which always causes a thoughtful pursing of lips among the more dour puritans from the hills.

There is a table with a hole in the middle through which a vine grew, allowing the resident Marquis to pluck his fruit fresh from the bough while broaching his meat. This has brought many a cry of envy from the visitors, as if a meal eaten without a canopy of verdure is a fraud. The library, when stocked, was a thing of glowing, gold-leaved joy, but the books have gone and the chamber, despite its magnificent woods, is nerveless and inert. There is a decorative motif of bronze monkeys in the centre of which precious stones once glittered, but the stones have been taken away and the monkeys just look bereft and sardonic about the whole business.

Flanking the castle and also available now to the ratepayers is a stretch of the most enchanting parkland which goes clear up to Llandaff, a curious wedge of medieval quietness stuck between the stridencies of Cardiff and the mining belt. The park has become a great lung of liberty for the young. On a Saturday morning a dozen school football teams can do their best in a setting of woodland to which autumn brings a beauty that would move a mule to tears. The castle peeps over the trees, a stronger heart than ever before for a fine, strong city. It is good when the past accepts and gives such a friendly handshake to the present.

from *A Welsh Eye* (1964)

HARRI WEBB

Answer from Limbo

Where will you spend eternity?
The posters question us.
The answer comes quite readily:
Waiting for a Cardiff bus!

Biographical Notes

Dannie Abse: b.1923, Cardiff. He studied at the Welsh National School of Medicine before moving in 1943 to London, where he continued his medical studies, qualifying as a doctor in 1950. He has published eight volumes of poetry, the most recent of which is *Ask the Bloody Horse* (1986), as well as plays, three novels and two volumes of autobiography, *A Poet in the Family* (1974) and *A Strong Dose of Myself* (1983). Tony Curtis has contributed an essay on Dannie Abse to the *Writers of Wales* series (1985).

Duncan Bush: b.1946, Cardiff. Educated at Warwick University and Wadham College, Oxford, he lives at St Donats in the Vale of Glamorgan. His verse has been published in three volumes: *Nostos* (1980), *Aquarium* (1983) and *Salt* (1985).

Gillian Clarke: b.1937, Cardiff. She read English at University College, Cardiff, and worked with the BBC in London before returning to her native city in 1960. Since 1975 she has been a freelance writer and edited *The Anglo-Welsh Review* from 1976 to 1984. Her most recent volume of poetry is *Letter from a Far Country* (1982) and her *Selected Poems* appeared in 1985.

Alexander Cordell (the pen-name of George Alexander Graber): b.1914, Colombo, Ceylon. He came to Wales in 1936 but went to live in the Isle of Man during the 1970s. His best-known novels are *Rape of the Fair Country* (1959) and *The Fire People* (1972).

Tony Curtis: b.1946, Carmarthen. Now resident in Barry he is Senior Lecturer at the Polytechnic of Wales. The author of four books of poetry, including his *Selected Poems* (1986), and editor of *The Art of Seamus Heaney* and *Wales: The Imagined Nation* (1986).

Roald Dahl: b.1916, Cardiff, where he attended Llandaff Cathedral School until he was nine. His enormously popular books for children include *Charlie and the Chocolate Factory* (1964), *The Twits* (1980) and *Revolting Rhymes* (1982).

Idris Davies (1905-53), was born in Rhymney, Monmouthsire. He left school at the age of fourteen to work underground, but later trained at Loughborough College as a teacher, holding posts in Llandysul, Cards., and Treherbert in the Rhondda Valley. His poems were published in four volumes during his lifetime: *Gwalia Deserta* (1938), *The Angry Summer* (1943), *Tonypandy* (1945) and *Selected Poems* (1953), and were collected in a single volume in 1972. There is an essay by Islwyn Jenkins about the life and work of Idris Davies in the *Writers of Wales* series (1972).

Tom Davies: b.1942, Pontypridd, Glamorgan, and brought up in Cardiff. He was educated at University College, Cardiff, and worked as a journalist with the *Western Mail*, *Sunday Times* and *The Observer* until 1980, when he became a full-time writer. Among his books are three novels: *The Electric Harvest* (1983), *One Winter of the Holy Spirit* (1984) and *Black Sunlight* (1986).

Siôn Eirian: b.1954, Hirwaun, Glamorgan, and brought up in Brynaman and

190

Mold. Educated at the University College of Wales, Aberystwyth, he is a freelance writer and has lived in Cardiff since 1975. He has published a volume of poetry, *Plant Gadara* (1975) and a novel, *Bob yn y Ddinas* (1979).

Peter Finch: b.1947, Cardiff. Since 1973 he has been the Manager of the Welsh Arts Council's Bookshop at Oriel in the city. He has published numerous volumes of verse, much of it experimental, and a collection of short stories, *Between 35 and 42* (1982). He edited the magazine *Second Aeon* from 1961 to 1974. His *Selected Poems* appeared in 1987.

W.J. Gruffydd (1881-1954), was born at Bethel, Caernarfonshire, and educated at Jesus College, Oxford, where he read Classics and English Literature. Appointed Lecturer in the Celtic Department of University College, Cardiff, in 1906, and Professor in 1918, he remained in that post until his retirement in 1946. He published several volumes of verse, including *Caniadau* (1932), edited three anthologies and wrote a number of scholarly works. From 1922 until 1951 he was editor of the literary magazine *Y Llenor*. A translation of his autobiography was published under the title *The Years of the Locust* (1976). Further details will be found in T.J. Morgan's essay in the *Writers of Wales* series (1970).

Douglas Houston: b.1947, Cardiff, but grew up in Scotland. Educated at the University of Hull, he returned to Wales in 1984 and now lives in Cwmbrwyno, near Aberystwyth. His first collection of poems, *With the Offal Eaters*, was published in 1986.

Emyr Humphreys: b.1919, Prestatyn, Flintshire. Educated at the University College of Wales, Aberystwyth, he has been a teacher, a drama producer with BBC Wales and a lecturer, but has been a full-time writer since 1972. He moved from Cardiff to live in Anglesey in 1985. He has published sixteen novels, including *A Toy Epic* (1958), *Outside the House of Baal* (1965) and a sextet collectively entitled *Land of the Living*, as well as four volumes of poetry and a study of historical themes, *The Taliesin Tradition* (1983). There is an essay on Emyr Humphreys by Ioan Williams in the *Writers of Wales* series (1980).

Geraint Jarman: b.1950, Denbigh, was brought up in Cardiff where he still lives. He is one of the best-known performers in the field of light entertainment in Wales today and a leading exponent of the reggae style in Welsh. Besides several recordings of his music, he has published two volumes of poetry, *Eira Cariad* (1970), and *Cerddi Alfred Street* (1976).

R.T. Jenkins (1881-1969), was born in Liverpool and brought up in Bala, Merioneth. He was a teacher in Cardiff before his appointment to a lecturer's post in the Department of Welsh History at the University College of North Wales, Bangor, in 1930, and later became Professor there. Most of his writings are on historical subjects but he also wrote short stories, a novella, *Orinda* (1943), an autobiography *Edrych yn ôl* (1968), and books for children. He was the editor of *The Dictionary of Welsh Biography* (1953). An essay on R.T. Jenkins by his former pupil Alun Llewelyn-Williams has appeared in the *Writers of Wales* series (1977).

Bobi Jones: b.1929, Cardiff. Brought up in an English-speaking home, he took a degree in Welsh at University College, Cardiff, in 1949, having learned the language at school. He has been Professor of Welsh at the University College of Wales, Aberystwyth, since 1980. One of the most prolific of Welsh writers, he has published seven volumes of poetry, as well as a very long poem, *Hunllef Arthur*, which appeared in 1986. He has also written two novels, five collections of short stories and numerous volumes of literary criticism and works of scholarship.

Glyn Jones: b.1905, Merthyr Tydfil, Glamorgan. He was a school-teacher in Cardiff from 1925 until his retirement in 1965. Among his books are three collections of short stories, two volumes of verse and three novels. His *Selected Short Stories* appeared in 1971 and his *Selected Poems* in 1975. An account of his early life and literary friendships appeared as *The Dragon has Two Tongues* in 1968. He was awarded an honorary doctorate by the University of Wales in 1974 in recognition of his achievement as a writer. There is an essay by Leslie Norris about his life and writing in the *Writers of Wales* series (1973).

Goronwy Jones, one of the pseudonyms of Dafydd Huws, b.1949, Bangor, Caernarfonshire. He has been a teacher of Welsh at St Illtyd's College, Rhymney, Cardiff, since 1972. A columnist in *Y Faner* and a script-writer for television, he is the author of *Dyddiadur Dyn Dwad* (1978).

Gwyn Jones: b.1907, Blackwood, Monmouthshire. Educated at the University College, Cardiff, he was appointed to a lecturer's post in the English Department of his old College in 1935. He was later Professor of English at the University College of Wales, Aberystwyth, and at Cardiff. His novels include *Times Like These* (1936) and *The Flowers beneath the Scythe* (1952). A volume of his *Selected Short Stories* appeared in 1974. He has also written extensively and authoritatively on the world of the Vikings, is the editor of several anthologies of verse and prose by Welsh writers and the translator of *The Mabinogion*. For further details see the monograph by Cecil Price in the *Writers of Wales* series (1976).

Harri Pritchard Jones: b.1933, Dudley, Worcestershire, but brought up in Anglesey. A doctor in Cardiff since the 1960s, he has published two collections of short stories, *Troeon* (1966) and *Pobl* (1978), and a novel entitled *Dychwelyd* (1972).

Jack Jones (1884-1970), was born in Merthyr Tydfil, Glamorgan, but settled in Cardiff during the 1920s, and was employed in a variety of jobs. A prolific writer, he published a dozen novels, including *Some Trust in Chariots* (1948) and *River out of Eden* (1951), as well as three volumes of autobiography, of which the finest is *Unfinished Journey* (1937). For further details see the essay by Keri Edwards in the *Writers of Wales* series (1974) and the account by Glyn Jones in *The Dragon has Two Tongues* (1968).

Eric Linklater (1899-1974), was born in Penarth, Glamorgan, and spent the first thirteen years of his life in Cardiff, before his family moved back to Scotland where his father had roots in Orkney. He was a prolific novelist and his best-known books are *Poet's Pub* (1929), *Juan in America* (1931) and *Private Angelo*

(1946).

Alun Llywelyn-Williams: b.1913, Cardiff. Educated at the University College, Cardiff, where he read Welsh and History, he later worked for the BBC and at the National Library of Wales. During the Second World War he served with the Royal Welsh Fusiliers. Appointed Director of Extra-Mural Studies at the University College of North Wales, Bangor, in 1948, he held a personal chair at the College until his retirement. He edited the literary magazine *Tir Newydd* from 1935 to 1939, and has published three volumes of verse, including *Golau yn y Gwyll* (1974), as well as several works of criticism and a volume of autobiography, *Gwanwyn yn y Ddinas* (1975).

R.M. Lockley: b.1903, Cardiff. He has described his distinguished career as a naturalist in about fifty books, including *Island Days* (1934) and *Letters from Skokholm* (1947), and his best-known work is *The Private Life of the Rabbit* (1965); he has also written novels. He left Wales in 1970 to live with his daughters in New Zealand.

Robert Minhinnick: b.1952, Neath, Glamorgan. He was educated at the University Colleges of Aberystwyth and Cardiff, and now lives in Porthcawl. His verse has been published in four volumes: *A Thread in the Maze* (1978), *Native Ground* (1979), *Life Sentences* (1983) and *The Dinosaur Park* (1985). For further details see *Common Ground: Poets in a Welsh Landscape* (ed. Susan Butler, 1985).

Jan Morris: b.1926, Clevedon, Somerset, was educated at Christ Church, Oxford. Formerly a journalist, she earns a living as a writer of travel books, and has also published a trilogy about the British Empire. She has lived in Wales for many years and has written memorably about the country, most notably in *The Matter of Wales: Epic Views of a Small Country* (1984).

Iorwerth C. Peate (1901-82), was born in the parish of Llanbrynmair, Montgomeryshire, and educated at the University College of Wales, Aberystwyth. He joined the staff of the National Museum of Wales in 1927 and became the first Curator of the Welsh Folk Museum. Besides studies of various aspects of folk-culture, he published essays, verse and two volumes of autobiography, of which *Rhwng Dau Fyd* (1976) is the more important. For further details see the monograph by Catrin Stevens in the *Writers of Wales* series (1986).

Alun Rees: b.1937, Merthyr Tydfil, Glamorgan. A journalist, he has worked for newspapers in London, including the *Sunday Telegraph*, but is now employed as a sub-editor by the *South Wales Echo* in Cardiff. His poems have been published in the volume *Release John Lucifer!* (1973).

Goronwy Rees (1909-79), was born at Aberystwyth, Cardiganshire, but brought up in Cardiff. He was a journalist before the Second World War and returned to academic life in 1951 when he joined the staff of All Souls College, Oxford. From 1953 to 1957 he was Principal of the University College of Wales, Aberystwyth, but resigned in acrimonious circumstances and spent the rest of his life in England. Besides three novels, and other books, he published two volumes of autobiography, *A Bundle of Sensations* (1960) and *A Chapter of Accidents* (1972) which are among his finest work.

Oliver Reynolds: b.1957, Cardiff. Educated at Hull University, he has written plays for children, and published one collection of his poems, *Skevington's Daughter* (1985). He recently came back to live in his native city.

Alun Richards: b.1929, Pontypridd, Glamorgan. He has been a probation officer, a sailor and a teacher, and lived for many years in Cardiff before moving to Swansea. Among his novels are *The Home Patch* (1966) and *Home to an Empty House* (1973) and his two collections of short stories are *Dai Country* (1973) and *The Former Miss Merthyr Tydfil* (1976). He has also written about rugby, the sea, and a volume of autobiography, *Days of Absence* (1986).

Bernice Rubens: b.1927, Cardiff, was educated at the University College in the city. She now lives in London. Among her dozen novels are *The Elected Member* (1969), *I Sent a Letter to my Love* (1975) and *Brothers* (1983).

Gilbert Ruddock: b.1938, Cardiff. Having learned the language at Cathays High School, Cardiff, he graduated in Welsh and was appointed Lecturer in the Welsh Department at University College, Cardiff, in 1969. His three volumes of verse are *Y Funud Hon* (1967), *Cwysi* (1973) and *Hyn o Iachawdwriaeth* (1985).

Howard Spring (1889-1965), was born in Cardiff, one of a gardener's nine children. He left school at the age of twelve and later became a journalist. His childhood is described in *Heaven Lies About Us* (1939). Among his best-known novels are *Shabby Tiger* (1934) and *Fame is the Spur* (1940). For further details see his two volumes of autobiography, *In the Meantime* (1942) and *And Another Thing* (1946).

Gwyn Thomas (1913-81), was born at Porth in the Rhondda Valley and educated at St Edmund Hall, Oxford. From 1942 to 1962 he taught Spanish at Barry. His novels include *The Alone to the Alone* (1947), *All Things Betray Thee* (1949) and *A Frost on my Frolic* (1953), and a volume of his *Selected Short Stories* appeared in 1984. His essays were collected in *A Welsh Eye* (1964) and *A Hatful of Humours* (1965), and *A Few Selected Exits* (1968) is largely autobiographical. His novel *Sorrow for thy Sons* was published posthumously in 1986. There is an essay on Gwyn Thomas by Ian Michael in the *Writers of Wales* series (1977); see also the album of photographs edited by Dai Smith in the *Writer's World* series (1986).

W.C. Elvet Thomas: b.1905, Fishguard, Pembrokeshire. He has lived in Cardiff for most of his life, his family having moved to the city when he was a few months old. Educated at the University College, Cardiff, he was a Welsh teacher at Cathays High School from 1931 until his retirement in 1969; Bobi Jones and Gilbert Ruddock are among those to whom he taught the language. He is the author of two books, one about Ireland, *Balchder Erin* (1978), and the other a volume of autobiography, *Tyfu'n Gymro* (1972).

John Tripp (1927-86), was born at Bargoed, Glamorgan, and brought up in Whitchurch, Cardiff. After working as a journalist in London, he returned to

Cardiff in 1969 to live as a freelance writer. Seven volumes of his verse were published during his lifetime, the last of which was *Passing Through* (1984); his *Collected Poems 1958-78* appeared in 1978. For further details see *Common Ground: Poets in a Welsh Landscape* (ed. Susan Butler, 1985).

Harri Webb: b.1920, Swansea. Educated at Magdalen College, Oxford, he worked as a bookseller in Cardiff after the Second World War and later as a librarian at Dowlais and Mountain Ash. His two most important collections of poetry are *The Green Desert* (1969) and *A Crown for Branwen* (1974).

Herbert Williams: b.1932, Aberystwyth. He is a freelance journalist and radio producer, working mainly for BBC Wales in Cardiff. He has published three volumes of poetry, including *The Trophy* (1967), as well as a verse-play, *A Lethal Kind of Love* (1968), and four books on historical subjects.

John Stuart Williams: b.1920, Mountain Ash, Glamorgan. He began his career as an English teacher at Whitchurch Grammar School, Cardiff, before becoming Head of the Department of English and Drama at the City of Cardiff College of Education in 1956. A critic with a special interest in modern Anglo-Welsh Literature, he has edited three anthologies and published four volumes of his own verse, including *Dic Penderyn* (1970) and *Banna Strand* (1975).

The editor, **Meic Stephens**, was born at Treforest, near Pontypridd, in 1938. He has lived in Cardiff for twenty years, but his family's connection with the city dates from 1900, when his grandparents met by chance in the Morgan Arcade. Educated at the University College of Wales, Aberystwyth, he was a French teacher and journalist before his appointment as Literature Director of the Welsh Arts Council in 1967. He founded *Poetry Wales* in 1965 and edited the magazine for eight years. A poet and editor of numerous books, he is the author of *Linguistic Minorities in Western Europe* (1976), a study of the interaction between culture and politics in sixteen states. He has also edited *The Oxford Companion to the Literature of Wales*, a major reference work published in 1986, and *A Book of Wales*, a selection of verse and prose.

Acknowledgements

Quotation on the back cover by kind permission of Frank Hennessey.

Extracts from *River out of Eden* (Hamish Hamilton, 1951) © the Estate of Jack Jones.

'A Celebration' was first published in *The Dinosaurs* (Christopher Davies Publishing Ltd, 1966); 'The Friend of Freedom' appeared in *Poetry Wales*; both © Herbert Williams.

Extract from *Brothers* (Hamish Hamilton, 1983), © Bernice Rubens.

Extract from *Peerless Jim* (Hodder & Stroughton, 1984), © Alexander Cordell.

Extract from *Heaven Lies About Us* (Grafton Publishers, 1956), © the Estate of Howard Spring.

Extract from *One Winter of the Holy Grail* (Macdonald, 1985) © Tom Davies.

Extract from *Fanfare for a Tin Hat* (Macmillan & Co Ltd, 1970) reprinted by permission of A.D. Peters & Co Ltd. on the behalf of the Estate of Eric Linklater.

Extract from *Myself when Young* (Andre Deutsch, 1979) © R.M. Lockley.

'Gwynt Traed y Meirw' appeared in *Green Rain* (Christopher Davies Publishing, 1967) © John Stuart Williams.

Translated extract from *Tyfu'n Gymro* (1972) by W.C. Elvet Thomas is reprinted by permission of Gwasg Gomer. © W.C. Elvet Thomas.

Translated extract from Alun Llywelyn-Williams' *Gwanwyn yn y Ddinas* (Gwasg Gomer, 1975) by permission of Luned Meredith and Gwasg Gomer. Translation of Alun Llywelyn-Williams' 'When I Was Young' is by Gwyn Williams, in whose *To Look for a Word* (Gwasg Gomer, 1976) it first appeared. Translation of Alun Llywelyn-Williams' 'Yesterday's Illusion' is by R. Gerallt Jones, in whose *Poetry of Wales 1930–1970* (Gwasg Gomer, 1974) it first appeared.

Extract from *A Chapter of Accidents* (Chatto & Windus, 1972) © the Estate of Goronwy Rees.

Extract from *The Dragon Has Two Tongues* (Dent, 1968), and 'The Common Path' © Glyn Jones.

Extract from *Boy* (Jonathan Cape Ltd, 1984) © Roald Dahl.

Translated extract from *Rhwng Dau Fyd* (Gwasg Gee, 1976) © the Estate of Iorwerth C. Peate.

Extract from *Times Like These* (Gollancz, 1936) by kind permission of Gwyn Jones.

'Cardiff Arms Park' was first published in *Poetry Wales*. © Alun Rees.

The three poems by Idris Davies are taken from his *Collected Poems* (Gwasg Gomer, 1972) © the Estate of Idris Davies.

Extracts from *The Best of Friends* (Hodder & Stroughton, 1978) and 'The Hero' from *Natives* (Secker & Warburg, 1968) © Emyr Humphreys.

Extract from W.J. Gruffydd's *Hen Atgofion* (Gwasg Gomer, 1936) is taken from D.M. Lloyd's translation *The Years of the Locust* (Gwasg Gomer, 1976) by kind permission.

Extracts from *Ash on a Young Man's Sleeve* (Hutchinson, 1964), *A Strong Dose of Myself* (Hutchinson, 1983), and the poems 'Return to Cardiff' and 'The Game' from *Collected Poems* (Hutchinson, 1977) © Dannie Abse.

ACKNOWLEDGEMENTS

'First Impressions' is previously unpublished, © Douglas Houston.
The translation 'Cardiff' by Joseph P. Clancy was originally part of a collection in Welsh, *Rhwng Taf a Thaf* (Christopher Davies Publishing, 1966), © Bobi Jones.
'Vigil' is a translation by the author of 'Gwylnos' from his *Storiau'r Dydd* (Gwasg Gomer, 1968) © Harri Pritchard Jones.
John Tripp's 'Captial' and 'Eglwys Newydd' are taken from *Collected Poems 1958–1978* (Christopher Davies Publishing, 1978); 'On Hayes Island' first appeared in *Planet*, © the Estate of John Tripp.
'You'll Not Move Me an Inch!' is an extract from 'The Scandalous Thoughts of Elmyra Mouth' a story in *Dai Country* (Michael Joseph, 1973) © Alun Richards.
The four poems by Gillian Clarke are all published in *Selected Poems* (Carcanet, 1985) © Gillian Clarke.
'Images from Tremorfa' by Robert Minhinnick was published in *Native Ground* (Christopher Davies Publishing, 1979); 'Dock' comes from *The Dinosaur Park* (Poetry Wales Press, 1985), © Robert Minhinnick.
The translations 'Daughters of the Dawn' and 'Down and Out' are of stories published in *Dyddiadaur Dyn Dwad* (Cyhoeddiadau Mei, 1978), © Dafydd Huws and Cyhoeddiadau Mei.
Duncan Bush's 'Back to Cardiff' was published in *Salt* (Poetry Wales Press, 1985); 'Three Voices' is previously unpublished. Both © Duncan Bush.
'Painters' by Peter Finch is previously unpublished. © Peter Finch.
'January Song' is a translation of 'Cân Ionawr' from *Cerddi Alfred Street* (Gwasg Gomer, 1976) © Geraint Jarman.
'My Square Mile' is a translated extract from *Bob yn y Ddinas* (Gwasg Gomer, 1979) © Sion Eirian.
'Wedding' is a translation of his own poem by Gilbert Ruddock. The original was published in *Cwysi* (Christopher Davies Publishing, 1973) © Gilbert Ruddock.
'Ddaeryddiaeth' is reprinted by permission of Faber & Faber Ltd from *Skevington's Daughter* by Oliver Reynolds.
'Fine Enough in it's Way' is an extract from Jan Morris's *The Matter of Wales* (Oxford University Press, 1984).
'Letter to John Tripp' is previously unpublished. © Tony Curtis.
'Quite a Place' is an extract from *A Welsh Eye* (Hutchinson, 1964) © the Estate of Gwyn Thomas.
'Answer from Limbo' was published in *Poems and Pints* (Gwasg Gomer, 1983) © Harri Webb.